D1197671

best ever

one pot

p

This is a Parragon Book
This edition published in 2004

Parragon
Queen Street House
4 Queen Street
Bath BA1 1HE
United Kingdom

Copyright © Parragon 2003

All rights reserved. No part of this publication may be reproduced,
stored in a retrieval system or transmitted, in any form or by any means,
electronic, mechanical, photocopying, recording or otherwise,
without the prior permission of the copyright holder.

Created and produced by
The Bridgewater Book Company Ltd,
Lewes, East Sussex

Photographer David Jordan
Home Economist Judy Williams
The publishers would like to thank Moulinex for lending the food processor
and Tower Pans for supplying the stainless steel saucepans and frying pans

ISBN: 1–40540-523-6

Printed in China

NOTE

This book uses metric and imperial measurements. Follow the same units
of measurement throughout; do not mix metric and imperial. All spoon
measurements are level: teaspoons are assumed to be 5 ml and tablespoons are
assumed to be 15 ml. Unless otherwise stated, milk is assumed to be full fat, eggs
and individual vegetables such as potatoes are medium, and pepper is freshly
ground black pepper.

The times given for each recipe are an approximate guide only because
the preparation times may differ according to the techniques used by
different people and the cooking times may vary as a result of the type of
oven used. Ovens should be preheated to the specified temperature. If using
a fan-assisted oven, check the manufacturer's instructions for adjusting the time
and temperature. The preparation times include chilling and marinating times,
where appropriate.

The nutritional information provided for each recipe is per serving or per portion.
Optional ingredients, variations or serving suggestions have not been included
in the calculations.

Recipes using raw or very lightly cooked eggs should be avoided
by infants, the elderly, pregnant women, convalescents and anyone
suffering from an illness.

contents

introduction

With today's hectic lifestyles, it is all too easy to resort to unhealthy and expensive takeaways and convenience foods. For a more economical and healthier alternative that is almost as easy, why not try one-pot meals for parties, Sunday lunches or family suppers? One-pot meals include everything from traditional soups and bakes to international dishes from Persia, Mexico and the Mediterranean and delicious alcoholic desserts – you will find a dish for every occasion.

Preparing food at home can give you a great sense of satisfaction, but it can seem something of a chore, and clearing up afterwards is often very tedious. If you have a busy life, one-pot meals may well be exactly what you need. Cook meals in batches and freeze, then heat in the microwave when you need them and relax for a few minutes. Running a household, holding down a job and feeding the family can be difficult to balance, and one-pot meals are the ideal time-saving solution. They make busy lives easier, make less mess in the kitchen and involve less chopping and peeling than many other dishes.

One-pot dishes also save on washing-up – they eliminate the need for a saucepan, frying pan, casserole and several serving dishes – most one-pot dishes can be served straight from the cooking pot. Try to find an attractive set of casseroles that you can serve from at the table, even when you have guests. One more advantage of not using serving dishes is that the food is kept piping hot, which saves you the fuss of warming plates in the oven.

Many one-pot meals can be frozen. Make them in large batches and freeze in family or single serving portions, depending on your household. Casseroles and stews are great for cooking in batches: double the ingredients (making sure your pot is big enough), and when the dish is ready, simply leave half to cool and then freeze in a rigid container or freezer bag. Soups will freeze well and can be kept for up to 3 months. To thaw, simply remove from the freezer 12 hours before you require the dish and leave at room temperature, or remove 24 hours before and place in the refrigerator.

the spice of life

One-pot meals need never be boring. The wonderful range of recipes featured here includes traditional stews and casseroles, perfect for winter evenings and large families. There are plenty of meat dishes, such as Irish Stew (see page 67) and Pork & Sausage Bake (see page 93) – hearty favourites guaranteed to fill you up. Fish is also featured, and you could serve Goan Fish Curry (see page 128) for a weekday supper, Cod in Lemon & Parsley (see page 121) for Sunday lunch or Swordfish with Tomatoes & Olives (see page 126) as a main course at a dinner party. There are dishes for vegetarian families or guests, such as Vegetable Chilli (see page 161), which makes a substantial lunch or dinner. Also impressive is Pasta with Garlic & Pine Kernels (see page 195), which would provide a delicious main course for meat-eaters too. Of course, not all one-pot meals have to be wintry casseroles, stews and pies – try Tricolour Pasta Salad (see page 194) as a summery lunch or alfresco meal, or make one of the risottos featured, such as Seafood Risotto (see page 187), for a warm picnic dish.

There are a surprising number of sweet one-pot dishes to serve for dessert. Try a substantial, warming dish to follow a light spring meal – complement Risotto Primavera (see page 189) with Pancake Pieces (see page 245).

A light summer meal eaten alfresco would be perfectly complemented by Forest Fruits Granita (see page 251) or Syllabub (see page 232).

Every cuisine in the world features one-pot dishes, proving how valuable and delicious they are. One-pot cooking preserves many of the nutrients that can disappear during boiling, grilling and roasting. They are usually cooked slowly over a long period of time, allowing the flavours and colours to mingle beautifully. Some of the recipes in this book are well known, such as British Cock-a-Leekie (see page 23), Irish Stew (see page 67), Pot-roast Pork (see page 83) and Flummery (see page 231), for example. Many American favourites are featured too, such as Quick Clam Chowder (see page 29), Brunswick Stew (see page 96), Louisiana Rice (see page 177) and Jambalaya (see page 184). Other dishes are more exotic, but this does not mean that they are harder to cook, and you should not be afraid to experiment with new flavours and ingredients. Try Chinese and south-east Asian methods of cooking, such as Hot & Sour Soup (see page 39) and Sweet & Sour Prawns (see page 148). Visit the other side of the world with Mexican Turkey (see page 115) and Chilli Con Carne (see page 56). Chicken Cacciatore (see page 103) is a well-known

Italian dish, while the Spanish Paella Del Mar (see page 132) is a variation on the classic chicken paella. Try one-pot dishes from Morocco, France, Thailand, Germany and Greece and find out which cuisine suits you – you never know, it may decide where you holiday next!

equipment

Investing in good-quality equipment is important. Poor quality pans and dishes do not cook food evenly, and are difficult to clean. The most important pans for one-pot cooking are casserole dishes, frying pans and saucepans. When making casseroles and pot roasts, you need a dish large enough to give the ingredients room to cook, but not so much room that they dry out.

If you are planning to cook lots of casseroles and stews, a flameproof casserole will be your best buy. A solid, heavy-based casserole can be expensive, but is worth the cost, as meals will be evenly cooked and flavoursome. A cast-iron casserole is best, but remember that they are very heavy when full.

Woks, frying pans and karahis (the Indian version of a wok) are also used for one-pot dishes, especially for stir-frying. Roasting tins are also important for cooking one-pot roasts, with the vegetables sizzling in the juices from the meat. You may prefer a non-stick lining, but whatever type you choose, make sure that it is solid and large, and that the sides are of an adequate height, or you may find that cooking juices drip dangerously over the rim.

You should think about the dishes you plan to cook and, therefore, the type of pan you will find most useful. If you cook on an electric hob with a flat surface, select a wok with a flat base, for example. A thick, solid base is important to allow even distribution of heat. If the manufacturer's instructions tell you to season a pan before use, do so, because this improves the quality of cooking and the pan's lifespan.

You will probably already have most of the other necessary utensils, but there may be some, such as a zester, that you might need to buy. Using a zester is far easier than trying to grate lemon or orange rind and then scrape it from the inside of the grater. They are inexpensive and readily available. Chopping boards are an essential item and will last a long time. Whether you prefer wood or plastic, select a good, solid board that will not slip easily. Remember to use a separate board for raw meat. It is now thought that you should avoid cleaning utensils with anti-bacterial products, as various strains of bacteria can become completely resistant. Hot soapy water is adequate for all pans and utensils; soak them first if there is burnt food on the base.

Measuring jugs and spoons with clear, easy-to-read numbers are essential. Although you can estimate amounts with many casseroles and stews, some dishes require exact measurements. Make sure you have a full set of imperial or metric measuring equipment and remember that the two systems are not interchangeable.

Other tools you will need include a slotted spoon for draining and serving – very valuable in one-pot cooking when you need to remove the meat ahead of the sauce. Try to find a good set of plastic utensils for non-stick surfaces or stainless steel for other dishes – these will last for years. A pestle and mortar is a necessity if you like to use fresh spices, which add a better flavour and colour than ready-ground ones.

Good-quality, sharp knives make life a lot easier, saving time and increasing safety in the kitchen. You should also buy a knife sharpener – using blunt knives is dangerous. A carving knife is ideal for carving pot roasts and other joints of meat. A large chopping knife with a heavy blade is useful for a multitude of purposes, but you may find a range of different knives suits you. A paring knife is smaller and lighter and is perfect for trimming, peeling and chopping small vegetables.

Nowadays, there are ways to speed up preparation times. For a real timesaver, invest in a food processor – a good-quality one will last for a long time. Alternatively, most supermarkets now stock a range of washed, peeled and chopped vegetables, such as carrots, baby sweetcorn, asparagus and salads, as well as canned goods. Canned foods are not so fresh as the ready-prepared varieties and often have little flavour and colour, but some types, such as tomatoes and pulses, are invaluable.

the storecupboard

Although fresh vegetables have a unique flavour and texture, there are alternatives that can make a delicious last-minute supper. Keep your storecupboard well stocked to prevent a last-minute rush to the supermarket. Ingredients in jars or cans will save on preparation time, too – most things can be bought chopped, peeled or flavoured at little or no extra cost. Improvise by using chickpeas when the recipe calls for kidney beans, and for new dishes experiment by using the ingredients buried at the back of the cupboard. Most of us have basics, such as pasta, rice and canned tomatoes, but next time you go shopping, spend some time in the canned food aisle and select a few more unusual ingredients to try.

canned pulses

Most canned pulses are excellent and avoid the lengthy soaking and cooking times needed for dried pulses. Chickpeas can be added to stews and casseroles towards the end of cooking to add substance and a mild, nutty flavour, or nearer the beginning for a richer flavour. Do not stir too much, as they may disintegrate, although they purée well to make a smooth soup or sauce. Experiment with adding chickpeas to your usual stuffing recipes. Dried chickpeas take a long time to prepare and there is not a noticeable difference in taste.

Red kidney beans are familiar to most people, usually from the Mexican Chilli Con Carne (see page 56), and can be added to any stew or casserole. Drain and rinse before adding to your cooking. They make a substantial meal and add an attractive splash of colour. Haricot beans are best known for their use in tomato sauce as baked beans.

Keep a can in the storecupboard and add to anything from salads to stews. Cannellini beans are white, and have a lovely buttery flavour. They make an interesting addition to casseroles and stews, and puréed cannellini beans can be used to thicken and lighten the colour of soups. Flageolet beans are pale green and are not strongly flavoured. They are a good choice for children. Their delicate taste will be overpowered in strongly flavoured dishes such as curries or stews – try them with salads and with subtly flavoured meat dishes.

fish

Canned tuna, salmon, anchovy fillets and sardines can be valuable storecupboard stand-bys. You can base a meal around them, or add them to a vegetable dish for extra flavour and colour. Use canned tuna in rice dishes, salads, pasta dishes and potato bakes. Use anchovies sparingly, as they have a strong, very salty flavour. Sardines are rather oily, but are very good for you and can be served straight from the can with a salad.

flavourings and sauces

Many flavourings used during cooking can also be put in a small dish at the table as a sauce, or drizzled over the dish before serving. Soy sauce is an Asian sauce made from fermented soya beans. Light soy sauce has a saltier, weaker flavour and colour than dark soy sauce – it should be used in a dish that requires no extra colouring. Dark soy sauce has a sweeter flavour, and adds an exotic colour to vegetable, rice and noodle dishes, as well as to meat – it should be used for heavy seasoning. No extra salt should be added to dishes with soy sauce in them.

Tabasco sauce is made in Louisiana. It can be added sparingly to soups and casseroles to add moderate heat, or in larger quantities to make very spicy chilli dishes. Traditional British sauces such as tomato ketchup, brown sauce and Worcestershire sauce can add flavour to casseroles. Add liberally to meat dishes.

Chutney is an ideal storecupboard ingredient. It can be used in obvious ways, such as in cheese sandwiches, but gives a great flavour to casseroles and soups. Try using it as a main ingredient in a stuffing, or add it to a pot roast.

noodles

An Asian alternative to pasta, noodles are healthy, convenient and quick to cook. They store well and keep for a long time. Use in soups and stir-fries, with sesame oil and soy sauce for the best flavour. Egg noodles are inexpensive and come dried, usually in rectangular cakes. Rice noodles, made from rice flour, are just as easy to cook. Cellophane noodles, also known as transparent, glass and bean thread noodles, are made from ground mung beans, and must be soaked before use. Most noodles are of medium thickness, although you may find thicker ones in an Asian supermarket. Long, thin noodles are best for soups and light sauces.

nuts

Most nuts stay fresh for a long time if sealed in an airtight container, although you must use pine kernels relatively quickly, as they have a high fat content and go stale. Try adding pine kernels to salads, stews, ice creams, sundaes and stuffings. They also make a very attractive garnish. Toast before using, as this improves the flavour. Peanuts can be used to garnish many dishes and are great for a satay sauce to go with whatever meat you have in the freezer. They are also useful as a snack for visitors, but bear in mind that nut allergies are common, and peanut allergies can be particularly dangerous.

oils

There are many different types of oil, but plain sunflower oil can be used for most purposes. It is more or less flavourless, so can be used in sweet and savoury dishes. Olive oil can be very expensive. Buy a lower quality oil – virgin or pure – if you intend to use olive oil for everyday cooking. Extra virgin olive oil is considered to be the best quality, and should be reserved for salad dressings and other dishes in which its flavour is intended to play a part.

For Asian cooking, sesame oil is particularly good. It has a strong taste, so use just a few drops for a stir-fry or in rice or noodle dishes for extra flavour. Use only at moderate temperatures, because it burns easily. It is often added at the end of cooking for extra flavour, rather than used as a frying oil.

Flavoured oils such as herb and garlic oils can be timesaving, because you don't have to chop fresh herbs and garlic separately. To make your own, add a few cloves of garlic and/or a handful of chopped, fresh herbs to a bottle of good-quality oil, seal and leave for at least a week to allow the flavours to release and infuse the oil.

olives and capers

Olives are invaluable as a snack, but they can also be incorporated into many dishes. Add them as a garnish or use them as a main ingredient in a dish; try black olives and stuffed green olives, which have different flavours. Both go well with fish, such as canned tuna and salmon. Similarly, capers can add a decorative touch. Add them sparingly to salads, as they have a strong, pickled flavour.

rice

There are many different types of rice. As well as the best known white long- and short-grain rices, you can also buy wild rice, risotto rice (such as arborio) and brown rice. Most dishes can be cooked with more than one type of rice, although some, such as risottos, have to be cooked with a specific type. Black glutinous and wild rice are dark in colour; wild rice is actually an aquatic grass. Red rice, such as Wahani from California and the semi-wild Camargue rice, has a pleasant flavour, and can make simple dishes look spectacular. Arborio, carnaroli and Vialone Nano are all types of round grain risotto rice. They absorb large quantities of liquid and are cooked by a particular method, resulting in the creamy but firm

texture unique to risotto. Brown rice has a nuttier texture than white rice. It takes longer to cook and will not swell as much, so you will need to use more of it.

tomatoes

Peeled, canned plum tomatoes add flavour, colour and substance to almost any meal, and add bulk to soups and sauces. Chopped sun-dried tomatoes preserved in oil are usually sold in jars and make a great stand-by base for sauces and pasta dishes. Add to casseroles and stews for a rich flavour, or to stuffings for colour and for a flavour that penetrates the meat. Use the flavoured oil as a salad dressing and to cook meats, especially chicken.

Tomato purée is very concentrated and you will need to add only a little to your cooking for a strong flavour and colour. Sun-dried tomato purée makes wonderful, flavoursome sauces. It has a darker colour than normal tomato purée and a stronger, more particular flavour, so use sparingly at first. If you use tomato purée regularly, buy a jar and store in the refrigerator.

Passata is an Italian alternative to canned tomatoes. It is made from sieved and puréed tomatoes and is smoother than canned tomatoes. It makes a great base for sauces and soups and can be added to casseroles and stews, with delicious results.

vinegars

It is worth experimenting with vinegars other than plain wine vinegar, as they all have unique flavours. You can make your own flavoured vinegars using the same method as for flavoured oil. Try herb or garlic vinegar – rosemary has a particularly delicious flavour. White wine vinegar can be used for everything from fish and chips to sauces, and is the best choice for salad dressings. Keep tightly sealed to avoid losing any of the flavour. Balsamic vinegar from northern Italy is darker in colour than most vinegars. Best used for salad dressings, balsamic vinegar is sometimes aged for up to 20 years, although you should buy a younger, less expensive vinegar for everyday use. Cider vinegar is made from apples and can make a lovely, summery salad dressing. It has a strong, very acidic flavour, and should be used sparingly.

making the most of one-pot dishes

An easy way to make the most of one-pot dishes is to serve them with a side salad of pasta or rice, or more conventional lettuce, cucumber and tomato. You can change the taste of a whole meal by adding a salad

dressing, either just before you serve, as a garnish, or at the table. Try strongly flavoured salad dressings, such as blue cheese with meat dishes, and lighter dressings such as vinaigrette with chicken and risottos.

Experiment with adding more unusual ingredients to salads, such as fruit, nuts, croûtons or lardons. Segments of orange add a lovely tangy flavour, as well as a splash of colour. Try adding fruit to a salad when serving with meat that traditionally goes well with fruit, such as duck or pork. Pine kernels, especially if they are toasted, make a quick and attractive addition and will not overwhelm the flavour of anything else. Croûtons are often flavoured with garlic and/or herbs and are best added to a salad served with a strongly flavoured dish. Add them just before serving, otherwise they tend to go soggy. If croûtons in your storecupboard go stale, sprinkle them with a little milk, spread out on a baking tray and bake in a preheated oven, 220°C/425°F/Gas Mark 7, for a few minutes, until crispy again – serve immediately. Ready-made lardons and croûtons are available in most supermarkets, and will retain their flavour and crispness as long as they are stored adequately.

Nowadays, many unusual and exotic types of salad leaves are available. Experiment with their different flavours, colours and textures. Try salads made with rocket, oakleaf, radicchio, mizuna and tatsoi, or combine these with more conventional leaves, such as cos, Little Gem and iceberg, and more conventional ingredients, such as tomatoes, radishes and beetroot for colour, and spring onions, shredded cabbage and anchovies for flavour. Baby spinach leaves also make good salads. Look at your storecupboard stand-bys for inspiration – try adding tuna, capers, a drizzle of balsamic vinegar and/or freshly grated Parmesan cheese.

Fresh herbs are a simple and attractive addition to salads. Try adding dill to a potato-based salad or a salad served with fish. A drizzle of olive oil and a handful of fresh, chopped herbs are all that is needed for many salads – chives are an excellent addition.

You can make your own salads of delicatessen quality at home, as well as plain lettuce and tomato salads. Pasta salad and rice salad can be made as a one-pot dish. Add any fresh vegetables that you have in the refrigerator – peppers, diced cucumber, beansprouts, grated carrot – and you can also add hard-boiled eggs, peanuts, sunflower seeds or cubes of cheese. You can make it up as you go along, and this can be one of the most enjoyable ways of preparing a meal. You can use potatoes and pulses as a basis for salads too. Mixed bean salad is delicious made with red kidney beans, cannellini beans and haricot beans, and is quick and easy to make. You can base your salad around any ingredients; try tomato salad with onions or coleslaw with sultanas.

Many salad dressings can easily be made at home and will keep quite well in the refrigerator. Their flavour will be superior to shop-bought versions, and you can eliminate the need for colourings, additives and preservatives. You can add a handful of chopped fresh herbs or other ingredients to a plain mayonnaise to adapt it to the dish you are serving. Try adding a handful of crumbled blue cheese, such as Stilton, to a plain mayonnaise and beat well, to make a strong and delicious accompaniment to stews and casseroles. Add freshly snipped chives or dill for a salad dressing, which will complement chicken, potatoes or fish. You can add anything – try sun-dried tomato or garlic oil in a dressing in place of the plain oil.

Bread is also a great accompaniment to most one-pot dishes, and can be served with or instead of a salad. Slices of basic white bread can be used for mopping up juices from stews, soups and casseroles, but many different and more interesting breads are now available. Most freeze well, and will keep for up to three months in the freezer. Remove and leave at room temperature about 24 hours before serving.

Most supermarkets and some smaller shops now have quite an extensive range of French bread, Italian bread and other more exotic breads. French bread is delicious served with soups, is inexpensive and looks attractive. Serve fresh and warm, if possible, with lots of butter and a side salad. Ciabatta and focaccia are Italian breads, most often baked with herbs. Both of these are ideal for serving with one-pot dishes with a lot of liquid, especially soups and stews. Improvise with the bread that is available in the shops, or bake it at home. Freeze a few different types of bread if your local supermarket has a good selection.

You can make an easy cheat's garlic bread by buying hot, fresh French bread if you live near a baker's. Make some garlic butter using soft, warm butter, a little garlic, herbs, and salt and pepper. Make vertical slits along the length of the bread with a sharp knife, then spread a little of the garlic butter inside the slits. Make sure the bread and butter are warm and that you use only a little garlic – it will taste stronger because it has not been cooked.

A simple way to liven up stews and casseroles and make them more substantial is to top them with bread and cheese. French bread works well, but you can use any bread that can be cut into thick slices. This is a great way to use up stale bread, as it works better than fresh bread. Cut the loaf into thick rounds or slices and spread with a thin layer of butter or olive oil. Thinly slice some cheese – Cheddar, Edam and Gruyère work well – and place some on top of each slice of bread. Towards the end of cooking, place the slices of bread and cheese on top of the casserole so that the bottom of the bread absorbs a little of the sauce and the cheese melts. Depending on your tastes, you may like to try placing a slice of tomato between the bread and cheese before cooking. If you are going to use oil instead of butter, a spray canister of oil ensures that you do not use too much. Alternatively, you could place a slice of bread and cheese in the base of each individual soup bowl before ladling in hot soup.

If you are making a one-pot soup and it looks too weak, try adding pâté to thicken it and add flavour. This works best with strongly flavoured soups, such as tomato, beef and lentil.

To add an attractive garnish to bowls of tomato soup and other dark-coloured soups, place a small spoonful of cream in the centre and run a cocktail stick through it to make a swirl. Soured cream or crème fraîche add a creamy texture and flavour to soups, and should be added towards the end of cooking to heat through.

desserts

Most one-pot desserts are a complete dish and don't need anything added. However, if you have a large family or a very hungry one, you may want to pad out the dish. The easiest thing to add to desserts is canned fruit – try a pineapple ring on top of each portion, or serve with a separate fruit salad. Try using canned mandarin segments, grapefruit or lychees, which go well with ice cream. Fresh fruit takes a little more preparation, and you have to bear in mind the time of year – will you be able to get fresh strawberries or blueberries?

Natural yogurt can be added to many desserts with a small bowl of sugar, honey or syrup at the table. Intensely flavoured honeys, such as orange blossom, are particularly delicious and are often attractive colours. Fruit-flavoured yogurts are cheap and quick, and can be added by the spoonful to the dessert or served separately in a bowl at the table.

Single cream is a classic with strawberries, raspberries and other fresh fruits, but for most other desserts, double cream or whipped cream is best. You can buy whipped cream in a spray form, saving time and effort, but this is not nearly as flavoursome or pleasant in texture as freshly whipped double cream. Crème fraîche is an alternative to cream – it is deliciously thick and creamy, and you will probably need only a small tub.

If you have a sweet tooth, try adding syrups or jams to your desserts. If you use a canned fruit for a dessert, reserve the syrup from the can to serve with another dessert the following day. Apricot jam goes well with pastries and pies, while blackcurrant and blueberry jams are delicious with baked dishes, such as muffins or scones. Dessert sauce can be bought in many flavours, such as chocolate, caramel, strawberry and raspberry, and is usually very sweet. Use as an alternative to syrups and jams when you run out – it keeps for ages.

Grate chocolate over a dish while it is still warm – much easier than melting chocolate in a bowl set over a saucepan of hot water. Grated chocolate is also delicious sprinkled over ice cream or cream and fresh fruit.

Ice cream and jelly are traditional children's favourites, but need not be limited to the little ones. Make adult jellies by adding a little alcohol and some fruit and serve with ice cream at an evening meal. To make children's jellies more interesting, add some edible treats at the base of the mould before leaving them to set, though these are not suitable for children under three.

basic recipes

mayonnaise

makes: about 200 ml/7 fl oz
preparation time: 15 minutes

1 egg
3 garlic cloves (optional)
150 ml/5 fl oz flavoured or plain oil
½ tsp cider vinegar
pinch of paprika
salt and pepper

1 Break the egg into a blender or food processor and add the garlic (if using). Process for 30 seconds.

2 Add a little oil, process, add a little more and process. Continue adding the oil until it is all incorporated and the mixture is thick, creamy and pale yellow.

3 Pour the mayonnaise into a bowl and gradually beat in the vinegar. Season with the paprika, salt and pepper.

vegetable stock

makes: about 2 litres/3½ pints
preparation time: 10 minutes
cooking time: 35 minutes

2 tbsp sunflower or corn oil
115 g/4 oz onions, finely chopped
115 g/4 oz leeks, finely chopped
115 g/4 oz carrots, finely chopped
4 celery sticks, finely chopped
85 g/3 oz fennel, finely chopped
85 g/3 oz tomatoes, finely chopped
2.25 litres/4 pints water
1 bouquet garni

1 Heat the oil in a saucepan. Add the onions and leeks and cook over a low heat for 5 minutes, or until softened.

2 Add the remaining vegetables, cover and cook for 10 minutes. Add the water and bouquet garni, bring to the boil and simmer for 20 minutes.

3 Sieve, cool and store in the refrigerator. Use immediately or freeze in portions for up to 3 months.

fish stock

makes: about 1.3 litres/2¼ pints
preparation time: 10 minutes
cooking time: 30 minutes

650 g/1 lb 7 oz white fish heads, bones and trimmings, rinsed
1 onion, sliced
2 celery sticks, chopped
1 carrot, sliced
1 bay leaf
4 fresh parsley sprigs
4 black peppercorns
½ lemon, sliced
1.3 litres/2¼ pints water
125 ml/4 fl oz dry white wine

1 Place the fish heads, bones and trimmings in a large saucepan. Add all of the remaining ingredients and bring to the boil, skimming off the foam that rises to the surface.

2 Reduce the heat, partially cover and simmer gently for 25 minutes.

3 Sieve the stock, without pressing down on the contents of the sieve. Cool and store in the refrigerator. Use immediately or freeze in portions for up to 3 months.

chicken stock

makes: about 2.5 litres/4½ pints
preparation time: 10 minutes
cooking time: 3½ hours

1.3 kg/3 lb chicken wings and necks
2 onions, cut into wedges
4 litres/7 pints water
2 carrots, roughly chopped
2 celery sticks, roughly chopped
10 fresh parsley sprigs
4 fresh thyme sprigs
2 bay leaves
10 black peppercorns

1 Place the chicken wings and necks and the onions in a large, heavy-based saucepan and cook over a low heat, stirring frequently, until lightly browned.

2 Add the water and stir thoroughly to scrape off any sediment on the base of the saucepan. Bring to the boil, skimming off any foam that rises to the surface. Add all of the remaining ingredients, partially cover and simmer gently for 3 hours.

3 Sieve, cool and place in the refrigerator. When cold, carefully remove and discard the layer of fat on the surface. Use immediately or freeze in portions for up to 6 months.

beef stock

makes: about 1.7 litres/3 pints
preparation time: 10 minutes
cooking time: 4½ hours

1 kg/2 lb 4 oz beef marrow bones, sawn into 7.5-cm/3-inch pieces
650 g/1 lb 7 oz stewing beef in 1 piece
2.8 litres/5 pints water
4 cloves
2 onions, halved
2 celery sticks, roughly chopped
8 peppercorns
1 bouquet garni

1 Place the bones in the base of a heavy-based saucepan and put the stewing beef on top. Add the water and bring to the boil over a low heat, skimming off any foam that rises to the surface.

2 Press a clove into each onion half and add to the pan with the celery, peppercorns and bouquet garni. Partially cover and simmer very gently for 3 hours. Remove the meat and simmer for 1 hour.

3 Sieve, cool and place in the refrigerator. When cold, carefully remove and discard the layer of fat on the surface. Use immediately or freeze in portions for up to 6 months.

soups

There is something especially appetizing about home-made soup, whether it is chunky and hearty, such as Bacon & Lentil Soup (see page 21), or delicate and fragrant, such as Avgolemono (see page 49). Most of the soups in this chapter make a filling first course or, served with some fresh rolls or crusty bread, a light lunch or evening snack.

It is worth making your own stock (see page 13) – and that's only one pot, too – because that way, you can be sure of the quality and flavour. Chicken stock is a good all-round basic, if you don't want to bother making several different types, and it can even be used for fish soups. If you do have to use stock cubes, look for ones with a low salt content and be careful when you season the soup.

The recipes incorporate all kinds of ingredients: an entire chicken supplies both the broth and the meat for two separate courses in the classic Scottish Cock-a-Leekie (see page 23) and a veritable market garden of vegetables is found in Italian Minestrone (see page 33). There are spicy soups from Asia, hearty country soups from France and fabulous fish soups from both America and the Mediterranean. There are familiar family favourites, such as Chicken Soup (see page 22), and some more unusual ideas, such as Sweetcorn, Potato & Cheese Soup (see page 45). All are easy to make and some are surprisingly quick, so you are sure to find one to please you and your family.

cabbage soup with sausage

cook: 1 hr 15 mins   **prep: 15 mins**   **serves 6**

NUTRITIONAL INFORMATION

Calories	.246
Protein	.15g
Carbohydrate	.21g
Sugars	.13g
Fat	.12g
Saturates	.4g

variation

If you wish, substitute any other meat stock, such as Beef Stock (see page 13), for the Chicken Stock in this soup.

Spicy or smoky sausages add substance to this soup, which makes a hearty and warming supper served with crusty bread and green salad.

INGREDIENTS

350 g/12 oz lean sausages, preferably highly seasoned

2 tsp olive oil

1 onion, chopped finely

1 leek, halved lengthways and thinly sliced

2 carrots, halved and thinly sliced

400 g/14 oz canned chopped tomatoes

350 g/12 oz young green cabbage, cored and roughly shredded

1–2 garlic cloves, finely chopped

pinch of dried thyme

1.5 litres/2¾ pints Chicken Stock (see page 13)

salt and pepper

freshly grated Parmesan cheese, to serve

cook's tip

If you don't have fresh stock, use water with 1 stock cube dissolved in it. Add a little more onion and garlic, plus a bouquet garni (remove it before serving).

1 Place the sausages in a large, saucepan and pour in enough water to cover generously and bring to the boil. Reduce the heat and simmer until firm. Drain the sausages and, when cool enough to handle, remove the skin, if you like. Slice thinly.

2 Heat the olive oil in a separate large, saucepan add the onion, leek and carrots and cook over a medium heat for 3–4 minutes, stirring constantly, until the onion begins to soften.

3 Add the tomatoes, cabbage, garlic, thyme, stock and sausages. Season to taste with salt and pepper. Bring to the boil, reduce the heat to low and cook gently, partially covered, for 40 minutes, or until the vegetables are tender.

4 Taste the soup and adjust the seasoning, if necessary. Ladle into warmed bowls and serve with the grated Parmesan cheese.

frankfurter & split pea broth

serves 6   **prep: 15 mins** ⟳   **cook: 2 hrs 30 mins** ⟳

*Economical, nourishing, filling and packed with flavour –
what more could you ask for on a chilly winter's evening?*

INGREDIENTS

225 g/8 oz salt belly of pork,
cut into cubes

2.5 litres/4½ pints water

500 g/1 lb 2 oz split peas, soaked in
enough cold water to cover for 2 hours

4 onions, chopped

2 leeks, chopped

4 carrots, chopped

4 celery sticks, chopped

1 cooking apple, peeled,
cored and chopped

1 tbsp muscovado sugar

1 bouquet garni

6 frankfurters, cut into
2.5-cm/1-inch lengths

25 g/1 oz butter

salt and pepper

celery leaves, to garnish

NUTRITIONAL INFORMATION	
Calories 614	
Protein 32g	
Carbohydrate 69g	
Sugars 17g	
Fat 25g	
Saturates 5g	

variation

Substitute other favourite vegetables,
such as parsnips and peppers, for the
carrots and celery, if you prefer.

cook's tip

You can use yellow or green
split peas for this soup. The
cooking time may vary
depending on their freshness
– the fresher they are, the
quicker they will cook.

1 Put the pork cubes into a large, heavy-based saucepan and add enough cold water to cover. Bring to the boil over a low heat, then drain well. Return the pork to the saucepan and add the water.

2 Drain and rinse the peas, then add them to the saucepan with the onions, leeks, carrots, celery, apple, sugar and bouquet garni. Bring to the boil, skimming off any scum that rises to the surface. Reduce the heat, cover and simmer, stirring occasionally, for 2 hours.

3 Remove and discard the bouquet garni and stir in the frankfurters and butter. Season to taste with salt and pepper and heat through. Ladle into warmed bowls, garnish with celery leaves and serve immediately.

bacon & lentil soup

cook: 1 hr 15 mins   **prep: 15 mins**   **serves 4**

NUTRITIONAL INFORMATION	
Calories 612
Protein 23g
Carbohydrate 26g
Sugars 7g
Fat 47g
Saturates 18g

variation

You can use different root vegetables, such as swede and parsnips, instead of the carrots and turnips, if you prefer.

Bacon and lentils have a real affinity – their flavours and textures complement one another. This popular family supper also includes a selection of tasty winter vegetables.

INGREDIENTS

450 g/1 lb thick, rindless smoked bacon rashers, diced
1 onion, chopped
2 carrots, sliced
2 celery sticks, chopped
1 turnip, chopped
1 large potato, chopped
85 g/3 oz Puy lentils
1 bouquet garni
1 litre/1¾ pints water or Chicken Stock (see page 13)
salt and pepper

cook's tip

Do not add any salt until the lentils have finished cooking, otherwise they will toughen, which will impair the texture of the soup.

1 Heat a large, heavy-based saucepan or flameproof casserole. Add the bacon and cook over a medium heat, stirring, for 4–5 minutes, or until the fat runs. Add the chopped onion, carrots, celery, turnip and potato and cook, stirring frequently, for 5 minutes.

2 Add the lentils and bouquet garni and pour in the water. Bring to the boil, reduce the heat and simmer for 1 hour, or until the lentils are tender.

3 Remove and discard the bouquet garni and season the soup to taste with pepper, and with salt, if necessary. Ladle into warmed soup bowls and serve immediately.

chicken soup

serves 4　　　**prep: 10 mins**　　　**cook: 30 mins**

A farmhouse classic, this delicious, hearty soup is packed with flavour, and makes a comforting one-pot meal. Serve with a generous side order of fresh, crusty bread.

INGREDIENTS

25 g/1 oz butter

1 small onion, finely chopped

1 leek, thinly sliced

4 skinless, boneless chicken thighs, diced

25 g/1 oz long-grain rice

850 ml/1½ pints Chicken Stock (see page 13)

1 tbsp chopped fresh parsley

salt and pepper

fresh parsley sprigs, to garnish

NUTRITIONAL INFORMATION

Calories	136
Protein	. . . . .10g
Carbohydrate	. . . . .7g
Sugars	. . . . .1g
Fat	. . . . .8g
Saturates	. . . . .4g

cook's tip

You can add other vegetables, such as diced carrot, with the onion and leeks in Step 1, or fresh beans or peas just before pouring in the stock in Step 2.

1 Melt the butter in a large, heavy-based saucepan. Add the onion and leek and cook over a low heat, stirring occasionally, for 5 minutes, or until softened. Add the chicken and cook over a medium heat for 2 minutes.

2 Add the rice and cook, stirring constantly, for 1 minute, or until the grains are coated with butter. Pour in the stock, bring to the boil, reduce the heat and simmer for 20 minutes, or until the chicken and rice are tender.

3 Stir in the parsley and season the soup to taste with salt and pepper. Ladle into warmed bowls, garnish with parsley sprigs and serve immediately.

cock-a-leekie

⏲ **cook: 2 hrs 45 mins**   ⏱ **prep: 15 mins**   **serves 6**

Two for the price of one – serve the soup separately as a first course and the meat and vegetables as a main course. Alternatively, for a really chunky dish, ladle the whole thing into large soup plates.

NUTRITIONAL INFORMATION	
Calories	348
Protein	21g
Carbohydrate	29g
Sugars	28g
Fat	18g
Saturates	6g

INGREDIENTS

1.3 kg/3 lb chicken

2.25 litres/4 pints Beef Stock (see page 13)

900 g/2 lb leeks

1 bouquet garni

salt and pepper

450 g/1 lb prunes, stoned and soaked overnight in enough cold water to cover

1 Put the chicken, breast-side down, in a large, heavy-based saucepan or flameproof casserole. Pour in the stock and bring to the boil, skimming off any froth that rises to the surface.

2 Tie half the leeks together in a bundle with kitchen string and thinly slice the remainder. Add the bundle of leeks to the saucepan with the bouquet garni and a pinch of salt, reduce the heat, partially cover and simmer for 2 hours, or until the chicken is tender.

3 Remove and discard the bundle of leeks and bouquet garni. Drain the prunes, add them to the saucepan and simmer for 20 minutes. Season to taste with salt and pepper and add the sliced leeks. Simmer for a further 10 minutes. Slice the chicken, or cut into bite-sized pieces, and serve immediately.

cook's tip

A bouquet garni usually consists of 3 fresh parsley sprigs, 2 fresh thyme sprigs and a bay leaf, tied together in a bundle.

beef & vegetable soup

serves 6　　　　　**prep: 20 mins**　　　　　**cook: 25 mins**

This colourful, spicy soup comes from South-east Asia, where it would be served with plain boiled rice, but it is substantial enough to make a filling meal on its own.

INGREDIENTS

2 tbsp groundnut or sunflower oil	1 litre/1¾ pints Chicken
1 large onion, finely chopped	or Beef Stock (see page 13)
115 g/4 oz fresh lean beef mince	salt
1 garlic clove, finely chopped	115 g/4 oz cooked peeled prawns
2 fresh red chillies, deseeded	225 g/8 oz fresh spinach, coarse stems
and finely chopped	removed and leaves shredded
1 tbsp ground almonds	175 g/6 oz baby corn cobs, sliced
1 carrot, grated	1 beef tomato, chopped
1 tsp muscovado sugar	2 tbsp lime juice
1-cm/½-inch cube shrimp	
paste (optional)	

NUTRITIONAL INFORMATION

Calories	140
Protein	. . . . .12g
Carbohydrate	. . . . .8g
Sugars	. . . . .6g
Fat	. . . . .7g
Saturates	. . . . .1g

variation

Replace the prawns with 55 g/2 oz of dried shrimp soaked in hot water for 10 minutes. Add the shrimp and soaking water with the stock in Step 2.

1 Heat the oil in a large, heavy-based saucepan. Add the onion and cook over a low heat, stirring occasionally, for 5 minutes, or until softened. Add the beef and garlic and cook, stirring, until the meat is browned.

2 Add the chillies, ground almonds, grated carrot and sugar. Add the shrimp paste (if using). Pour in the stock and season to taste with salt. Bring the mixture to the boil over a low heat, then simmer for 10 minutes.

3 Stir in the prawns, spinach, corn cobs, tomato and lime juice. Simmer the mixture for a further 2–3 minutes, or until heated through. Ladle into warmed bowls and serve immediately.

cook's tip

Shrimp paste, also known as blachan and terasi, is available from Chinese food stores. Before use, wrap a cube of it in foil and place in a frying pan over a low heat, turning occasionally, for 5 minutes.

scotch broth

cook: 1 hr 30 mins   **prep: 10–15 mins**   **serves 4**

NUTRITIONAL INFORMATION

Calories 186

Protein 13g

Carbohydrate 23g

Sugars 6g

Fat 5g

Saturates 2g

variation

Replace the swede with the same amount of turnip and substitute the parsnip with potato, if you prefer.

This traditional winter soup is full of goodness, with lots of tasty golden vegetables along with tender barley and lamb.

INGREDIENTS

55 g/2 oz pearl barley	1 bay leaf
300 g/10½ oz lean boneless lamb, such	1 large leek, quartered lengthways
as shoulder or neck fillet, trimmed of	and sliced
fat and cut into 1-cm/½-inch cubes	2 large carrots, finely diced
700 ml/1¼ pints water	1 parsnip, finely diced
2 garlic cloves, finely chopped	125 g/4½ oz swede, diced
or crushed	salt and pepper
1 litre/1¾ pints Chicken Stock	2 tbsp chopped fresh parsley
(see page 13)	fresh parsley sprigs, to garnish
1 onion, finely chopped	crusty bread, to serve

cook's tip

This soup is lean when the lamb is trimmed. By making it beforehand and chilling in the refrigerator, you can remove any hardened fat before reheating it.

1 Rinse the barley under cold running water. Place in a large, heavy-based saucepan and pour in enough water to cover. Bring to the boil over a medium heat and boil for 3 minutes, skimming off any foam that rises to the surface. Remove the saucepan from the heat, cover and reserve until required.

2 Place the lamb in a separate large, heavy-based saucepan with the water and bring to the boil. Skim off any foam that rises to the surface. Stir in the garlic, stock, onion and bay leaf. Reduce the heat, partially cover and simmer for 15 minutes.

3 Drain the barley and add to the soup.

Add the leek, carrots, parsnip and swede. Simmer, stirring occasionally, for 1 hour, or until the lamb and vegetables are cooked.

4 Season to taste with salt and pepper and stir in the chopped parsley. Ladle into warmed serving bowls, garnish with parsley sprigs and serve with crusty bread.

quick clam chowder

cook: 35 mins   **prep: 10 mins**   **serves 4**

NUTRITIONAL INFORMATION

Calories	.356
Protein	24g
Carbohydrate	.23g
Sugars	.7g
Fat	.19g
Saturates	.8g

variation

If you like, add 1–2 fresh red chillies, deseeded and sliced, to the saucepan in Step 2 and then continue as in the main recipe.

There are many versions of this classic, rich shellfish soup from America. New England chowder uses milk rather than stock and has no tomatoes. This is a version of Manhattan clam chowder.

INGREDIENTS

2 tsp sunflower oil

115 g/4 oz rindless streaky bacon, diced

25 g/1 oz butter

1 onion, chopped

2 celery sticks, chopped

2 potatoes, chopped

salt and pepper

2 leeks, sliced

400 g/14 oz canned chopped tomatoes

3 tbsp chopped fresh parsley

1.2 litres/2 pints Fish Stock (see page 13)

550 g/1 lb 4 oz canned clams, drained and rinsed

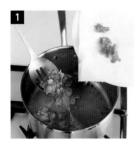

cook's tip

Canned clams are available all year round from most large supermarkets. They take the effort out of preparing clam chowder, and make a quick, easy and unusual soup.

1 Heat the oil in a heavy-based saucepan. Add the bacon and cook over a medium heat, stirring, for 5 minutes, or until the fat runs and it begins to crisp. Remove from the saucepan, drain on kitchen paper and reserve.

2 Add the butter to the saucepan and stir to melt. Add the onion, celery and potatoes with a pinch of salt. Cover and cook over a low heat, stirring occasionally, for 10 minutes, or until soft.

3 Stir in the leeks, the tomatoes and their juices and 2 tablespoons of the parsley. Pour in the stock, bring to the boil, reduce the heat and simmer for 10–15 minutes, or until the

vegetables are tender. Season to taste with salt and pepper and stir in the clams. Heat the soup through gently for 2–3 minutes, then ladle into warmed bowls, garnish with the remaining parsley and reserved bacon and serve.

genoese fish soup

serves 4 **prep: 15 mins** ⟲ **cook: 25 mins** ⟳

You can use any firm white fish fillets for this tasty soup. The best way to remove any small bones is to pull them out with tweezers before you begin chopping the flesh.

INGREDIENTS

25 g/1 oz butter

1 onion, chopped

1 garlic clove, finely chopped

55 g/2 oz rindless streaky bacon, diced

2 celery sticks, chopped

400 g/14 oz canned chopped tomatoes

150 ml/5 fl oz dry white wine

300 ml/10 fl oz Fish Stock (see page 13)

4 fresh basil leaves, torn

2 tbsp chopped fresh
flat-leaved parsley

salt and pepper

450 g/1 lb white fish fillets, such as cod
or monkfish, skinned and chopped

115 g/4 oz cooked peeled prawns

NUTRITIONAL INFORMATION	
Calories	.276
Protein	30g
Carbohydrate	.7g
Sugars	.5g
Fat	.12g
Saturates	.6g

variation

You could also use haddock, ling or sea bass to make this dish. If you are on a budget, coley would make a cheaper alternative.

cook's tip

Monkfish is a good choice for this soup, as it has only a single central bone down the tail. Make sure you peel off the grey membrane from the flesh before chopping and cooking.

1 Melt the butter in a large, heavy-based saucepan. Add the chopped onion and garlic and cook over a low heat, stirring occasionally, for 5 minutes, or until softened.

2 Add the streaky bacon and celery and cook, stirring frequently, for a further 2 minutes.

3 Add the tomatoes and their juices, the wine, stock, basil and 1 tablespoon of the parsley. Season to taste with salt and pepper. Bring to the boil, then reduce the heat and simmer for 10 minutes.

4 Add the fish and cook for 5 minutes, or until it is opaque. Add the prawns and heat through gently for 3 minutes. Ladle into a warmed tureen, garnish with the remaining chopped parsley and serve immediately.

minestrone

cook: 1 hr 30 mins–2 hrs　　**prep: 15 mins**　　serves 4

NUTRITIONAL INFORMATION

Calories 440

Protein 18g

Carbohydrate 67g

Sugars 16g

Fat 13g

Saturates 3g

variation

Although the haricot beans are a traditional ingredient for this soup, you could substitute cannellini or pinto beans, if you prefer.

Ever-popular, this fabulous Italian soup contains a cornucopia of fresh and dried vegetables – virtually every Italian cook has their own personal version of the recipe.

INGREDIENTS

3 tbsp olive oil

2 onions, chopped

½ small green or Savoy cabbage, thick stalks removed and leaves shredded

2 courgettes, chopped

2 celery sticks, chopped

2 carrots, chopped

2 potatoes, chopped

4 large tomatoes, peeled and chopped

115 g/4 oz dried haricot beans, soaked overnight in enough cold water to cover

1.2 litres/2 pints Chicken or Vegetable Stock (see page 13)

115 g/4 oz dried soup pasta

salt and pepper

freshly shaved Parmesan cheese, to garnish

4 tbsp freshly grated Parmesan cheese, to serve

cook's tip

It is not absolutely necessary to use a flavoured stock for this soup. If you want to make minestrone without making stock, just substitute the same amount of water.

1 Heat the oil in a large, heavy-based saucepan. Add the onions and cook over a low heat, stirring occasionally, for 5 minutes, or until softened.

2 Add the cabbage, courgettes, celery, carrots, potatoes and tomatoes to the saucepan, cover and cook, stirring occasionally, for 10 minutes.

3 Drain and rinse the beans, then add to the saucepan. Pour in the stock, bring to the boil, cover and simmer for 1–1½ hours, or until the beans are tender.

4 Add the soup pasta to the saucepan and cook, uncovered, for 8–10 minutes, or until tender but still firm to the bite. Season to taste with salt and pepper and ladle into warmed bowls. Garnish with fresh Parmesan cheese shavings and an extra sprinkling of pepper. Serve, handing the grated Parmesan cheese separately.

indian potato & pea soup

serves 4   **prep: 5 mins** ⟳   **cook: 35 mins** ⟳

A slightly hot and spicy Indian flavour is given to this soup with the use of garam masala, chilli, cumin and coriander – ideal for warming up a chilly winter's evening.

INGREDIENTS

2 tbsp vegetable oil

225 g/8 oz floury potatoes, diced

1 large onion, chopped

2 garlic cloves, crushed

1 tsp garam masala

1 tsp ground coriander

1 tsp ground cumin

850 ml/1½ pints Vegetable Stock
(see page 13)

1 fresh red chilli, deseeded and chopped

100 g/3½ oz frozen peas

4 tbsp natural yogurt

salt and pepper

chopped fresh coriander, to garnish

NUTRITIONAL INFORMATION	
Calories 153	
Protein 6g	
Carbohydrate 18g	
Sugars 6g	
Fat 6g	
Saturates 1g	

cook's tip

Always wash your hands after handling chillies because they contain volatile oils that can irritate the skin and make your eyes and lips burn if you touch your face after chopping them.

1 Heat the vegetable oil in a large, heavy-based saucepan. Add the potatoes, onion and garlic and sauté over a low heat, stirring constantly, for 5 minutes.

2 Add the garam masala, ground coriander and cumin and cook, stirring constantly, for 1 minute, then stir in the Vegetable Stock and chilli and bring the mixture to the boil. Reduce the heat, cover and simmer for 20 minutes, or until the potatoes begin to break down.

3 Add the peas and cook for a further 5 minutes. Stir in the yogurt and season to taste with salt and pepper.

Ladle into warmed soup bowls, garnish with chopped fresh coriander and serve.

mushroom & ginger soup

cook: 15 mins

prep: 10 mins, plus 30 mins soaking (optional)

serves 4

Thai soups are very quickly and easily put together, and are cooked so that each ingredient can still be tasted in the finished dish. The noodles make the soup into a meal in itself.

NUTRITIONAL INFORMATION	
Calories	.74
Protein	.3g
Carbohydrate	.9g
Sugars	.1g
Fat	.3g
Saturates	.0.4g

INGREDIENTS

15 g/½ oz dried Chinese mushrooms or
125 g/4½ oz field or chestnut mushrooms
1 litre/1¾ pints hot Vegetable Stock
(see page 13)
125 g/4½ oz thread egg noodles
2 tsp sunflower oil
3 garlic cloves, crushed
2.5-cm/1-inch piece fresh root ginger,
finely shredded
½ tsp mushroom ketchup
1 tsp light soy sauce
125 g/4½ oz beansprouts
fresh coriander sprigs, to garnish

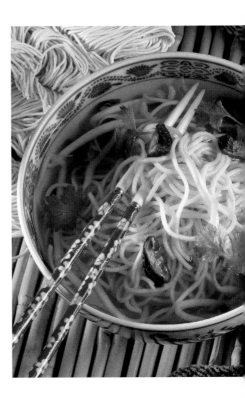

cook's tip

If you are on a low-fat diet, substitute rice noodles for the egg noodles. They contain no fat, and are an ideal way to bulk out a thin soup.

1 Soak the dried Chinese mushrooms (if using) for at least 30 minutes in 300 ml/10 fl oz of the hot stock. Drain the mushrooms and reserve the stock. Remove the stalks of the mushrooms and discard. Slice the caps and reserve. Cook the noodles for 2–3 minutes in boiling water, then drain and rinse. Reserve until required.

2 Heat the sunflower oil in a preheated wok or large, heavy-based frying pan over a high heat. Add the garlic and ginger, stir and add the mushrooms. Stir over a high heat for 2 minutes.

3 Add the remaining Vegetable Stock with the reserved stock and bring to the boil. Add the mushroom ketchup and soy sauce. Stir in the beansprouts and cook until tender. Place some noodles in each soup bowl and ladle the soup on top. Garnish with fresh coriander sprigs and serve immediately.

green vegetable soup

serves 6 **prep: 20 mins** **cook: 50 mins**

This soup takes advantage of a medley of summer vegetables bursting with seasonal flavour. If you find fresh flageolets or other fresh beans, be sure to include them.

INGREDIENTS

1 tbsp olive oil

1 onion, finely chopped

1 large leek, split and thinly sliced

1 celery stick, thinly sliced

1 carrot, quartered and thinly sliced

1 garlic clove, finely chopped

1.4 litres/2½ pints water

1 potato, diced

1 parsnip, finely diced

1 small kohlrabi, diced

150 g/5½ oz French beans, cut into small pieces

150 g/5½ oz fresh or frozen peas

400 g/14 oz canned flageolet beans, drained and rinsed

2 small courgettes, quartered and sliced

salt and pepper

100 g/3½ oz spinach leaves, shredded

PESTO

1 large garlic clove, finely chopped

15 g/½ oz basil leaves

4 tbsp extra virgin olive oil

85 g/3 oz freshly grated Parmesan cheese

NUTRITIONAL INFORMATION

Calories	.260
Protein	.12g
Carbohydrate	.21g
Sugars	.7g
Fat	.15g
Saturates	.4g

variation

If you cannot find a kohlrabi to use in this soup, substitute diced turnip where the kohlrabi is added in Step 2.

cook's tip

You do not have to use a blender or food processor to make pesto. Grinding the ingredients together with a pestle and mortar will work just as well.

1 Heat the olive oil in a large, heavy-based saucepan. Add the onion and leek and cook over a low heat, stirring occasionally, for 5 minutes. Add the celery, carrot and garlic, cover and cook for a further 5 minutes.

2 Add the water, potato, parsnip, kohlrabi and French beans. Bring to the boil, reduce the heat, cover and simmer for 5 minutes. Add the peas, flageolet beans and courgettes and season to taste with salt and pepper. Cover and simmer for 25 minutes, or until the vegetables are tender.

3 Meanwhile, make the pesto. Place all of the ingredients in a blender or food processor, reserving a few basil leaves for the garnish. Process until smooth, then reserve until required.

4 Add the spinach to the soup and simmer for 5 minutes. Stir in a spoonful of the pesto. Ladle the soup into warmed soup bowls, garnish with the reserved basil leaves and hand round the remaining pesto separately.

hot & sour soup

cook: 10 mins

prep: 10 mins, plus 20 mins soaking

serves 6

NUTRITIONAL INFORMATION

Calories 120

Protein 7g

Carbohydrate 17g

Sugars 2g

Fat 3g

Saturates 2g

In a typically Chinese approach, the flavours of this spicy Eastern soup are perfectly balanced, and are brought together in a harmonious blend of complementary colours and textures.

INGREDIENTS

6 dried Chinese mushrooms

15 g/½ oz cloud ears (see Cook's Tip)

1.5 litres/2¾ pints Chicken Stock (see page 13)

4 tbsp rice wine vinegar

2 tsp chilli sauce

1 tbsp dark soy sauce

1 tbsp Chinese rice wine

1 garlic clove, finely chopped

2 tsp finely chopped fresh root ginger

1 carrot, cut into thin strips

175 g/6 oz canned bamboo shoots, drained, rinsed and cut into thin strips

225 g/8 oz firm tofu (drained weight)

2 tbsp cornflour

3 tbsp water

4 spring onions, thinly sliced diagonally, to garnish

variation

If you cannot find any Chinese rice wine for this soup, substitute dry sherry, which works almost as well.

cook's tip

Cloud ears, Chinese fungi that grow on trees, are available from Chinese food stores. They are used in soup, more for texture than flavour. The similar wood ears feature in stir-fries and fish dishes.

1 Place the mushrooms and cloud ears in separate bowls, then add enough boiling water to each bowl to cover. Leave to soak for 20 minutes. Drain the mushrooms, then remove and discard the stems and thinly slice the caps. Drain and rinse the cloud ears, then cut off any woody parts and thinly slice the rest.

2 Heat the stock in a large saucepan. Add the mushrooms, cloud ears, vinegar, chilli sauce, soy sauce, Chinese rice wine, garlic, ginger, carrot and bamboo shoots. Bring the mixture to the boil.

3 Meanwhile, cut the tofu into thin slices and reserve. Combine the cornflour and water to make a smooth paste. Stir the paste into the boiling soup, reduce the heat and simmer, stirring constantly, for 3 minutes, or until slightly thickened. Stir in the tofu and heat through. Ladle the soup into warmed bowls, garnish with the spring onions and serve immediately.

mulligatawny soup

serves 4 **prep: 20 mins** **cook: 1 hr 45 mins–2 hrs**

Redolent of the days of the British Raj, this spicy soup was imported by colonials returning home from India. The sun has long since set on the Empire, but this 'pepper water' remains a perennial favourite.

INGREDIENTS

4 tbsp groundnut or sunflower oil

2 chicken pieces, about 350 g/12 oz each

1 onion, chopped

1 carrot, chopped

1 turnip, chopped

1 tbsp curry paste

8 black peppercorns, crushed

4 cloves

55 g/2 oz red split lentils

850 ml/1½ pints Chicken Stock (see page 13)

4 tbsp sultanas

salt

fresh coriander sprigs, to garnish

NUTRITIONAL INFORMATION	
Calories	329
Protein	14g
Carbohydrate	36g
Sugars	28g
Fat	15g
Saturates	2g

variation

Omit the sultanas. Add 1 cored, sliced cooking apple with the vegetables and 1 tablespoon of desiccated coconut with the spices in Step 2.

cook's tip

Curry paste is made from a mixture of spices, such as turmeric, fenugreek and cumin. It comes in varying levels of spicy heat, so check you have chosen your preferred strength before you purchase.

1 Heat the oil in a large, heavy-based saucepan. Add the chicken and cook over a medium heat, turning frequently, for 10–15 minutes, or until golden brown all over. Transfer the chicken to a plate and reserve.

2 Add the vegetables to the saucepan and cook, stirring occasionally, for 10 minutes, or until just beginning to colour. Stir in the curry paste, peppercorns and cloves and cook, stirring constantly, for 1 minute.

3 Stir in the lentils, pour in the stock and bring to the boil. Return the chicken to the pan with the sultanas, cover and simmer over a low heat for 1¼–1½ hours.

4 Remove the chicken from the saucepan. Remove and discard the skin and cut the flesh into bite-sized pieces. Return them to the saucepan to heat through and season to taste with salt. Ladle the soup into warmed bowls, garnish with fresh coriander sprigs and serve.

umbrian onion soup

serves 4   **prep: 20 mins**   **cook: 1 hr**

Like traditional Genoese Fish Soup (see page 30), this is a substantial and warming country soup which originally comes from northern Italy. Serve it with plenty of fresh, crusty bread.

INGREDIENTS

700 g/1 lb 9 oz onions

115 g/4 oz rindless streaky bacon or pancetta, chopped

25 g/1 oz unsalted butter

2 tbsp olive oil

2 tsp sugar

salt and pepper

1.2 litres/2 pints Chicken Stock (see page 13)

350 g/12 oz plum tomatoes, peeled and chopped

12 fresh basil leaves

freshly grated Parmesan cheese, to serve

NUTRITIONAL INFORMATION

Calories	300
Protein	7g
Carbohydrate	19g
Sugars	15g
Fat	23g
Saturates	9g

cook's tip

The best onions to use for this soup are sweet white Italian onions. These have a very mild flavour, which complements the other ingredients perfectly.

1 Thinly slice the onions and reserve. Place the bacon in a large, heavy-based saucepan and cook over a low heat, stirring, for 5 minutes, or until the fat begins to run. Add the butter, olive oil, sliced onions, sugar and a pinch of salt and stir to mix. Cover and cook, stirring occasionally, for 15–20 minutes, or until the onions are golden brown.

2 Pour in the stock, add the tomatoes and season to taste with salt and pepper. Cover and simmer, stirring occasionally, for 30 minutes.

3 Tear 8 of the basil leaves into pieces and stir into the soup, then taste and adjust the seasoning, if necessary. Ladle the soup into warmed bowls, garnish with the remaining basil leaves and serve, handing the Parmesan cheese round separately.

potato, carrot & leek soup

cook: 45 mins   **prep: 10 mins**   **serves 4**

Once you have tried this thick, rich, substantial soup, it is sure to become a family favourite for its creamy taste and velvety texture. There is also an added bonus – it is easy and inexpensive to make.

NUTRITIONAL INFORMATION	
Calories 317	
Protein 5g	
Carbohydrate 31g	
Sugars 9g	
Fat 20g	
Saturates 13g	

INGREDIENTS

25 g/1 oz butter

3 potatoes, chopped

3 carrots, chopped

3 leeks, chopped

1.2 litres/2 pints Chicken Stock
(see page 13)

½ tsp sugar

½ tsp freshly grated nutmeg

salt and pepper

3 tbsp double cream, plus extra
to garnish

cook's tip

This soup is also delicious made with leftover stock from boiling a side of bacon or gammon, or made with Beef Stock (see page 13).

1 Melt the butter in a large, heavy-based saucepan. Add the potatoes, carrots and leeks and cook over a low heat, stirring occasionally, for 10 minutes.

2 Pour in the stock and bring to the boil. Reduce the heat, partially cover the saucepan and simmer for 30 minutes, or until the vegetables are tender. Remove from the heat and leave to cool slightly.

3 Pour the mixture into a blender or food processor and process until smooth. Return the soup to the rinsed-out saucepan, then stir in the sugar and nutmeg and season to taste with salt and pepper. Return to the heat and stir in the cream. Ladle the soup into warmed bowls and serve immediately, garnished with a swirl of cream on top.

sweetcorn, potato & cheese soup

cook: 12–15 mins   **prep: 20 mins**   **serves 4**

NUTRITIONAL INFORMATION

Calories 860

Protein 16g

Carbohydrate 54g

Sugars 15g

Fat 66g

Saturates 41g

variation

If you can't find fresh sage, substitute a pinch of dried sage for the chopped leaves in Step 3 and omit the garnish.

This easy-to-make, satisfying soup is put together with mainly storecupboard ingredients. It is the perfect choice for a Sunday brunch, as it takes very little effort or concentration.

INGREDIENTS

25 g/1 oz butter

2 shallots, finely chopped

225 g/8 oz potatoes, diced

4 tbsp plain flour

2 tbsp dry white wine

300 ml/10 fl oz milk

325 g/11½ oz canned sweetcorn, drained

85 g/3 oz Gruyère, Emmenthal or Cheddar cheese, grated

8–10 fresh sage leaves, chopped

425 ml/15 fl oz double cream

fresh sage sprigs, to garnish

CROUTONS

2–3 slices of day-old white bread

2 tbsp olive oil

cook's tip

When you are cooking croûtons, make sure the oil is very hot before adding the bread cubes, otherwise the cubes may turn out soggy rather than crisp.

1 To make the croûtons, cut the crusts off the bread slices, then cut the remaining bread into 5-mm/ ¼-inch squares. Heat the olive oil in a heavy-based frying pan and add the bread cubes. Cook, tossing and stirring constantly, until evenly coloured. Drain the croûtons thoroughly on kitchen paper and reserve.

2 Melt the butter in a large, heavy-based saucepan. Add the shallots and cook over a low heat, stirring occasionally, for 5 minutes, or until softened. Add the potatoes and cook, stirring, for 2 minutes.

3 Sprinkle in the flour and cook, stirring, for 1 minute. Remove the saucepan from the heat and stir in the white wine, then gradually stir in the milk. Return the saucepan to the heat and bring to the boil stirring constantly, then reduce the heat and simmer.

4 Stir in the sweetcorn kernels, grated cheese, chopped sage and cream and heat through gently until the cheese has just melted. Ladle the soup into warmed bowls, scatter over the croûtons, garnish with fresh sage sprigs and serve immediately.

roasted vegetable soup

serves 6 **prep: 15 mins, plus 10 mins cooling** **cook: 1 hr 10 mins**

Mediterranean vegetables, roasted in olive oil and flavoured with thyme, are the basis for this delicious, creamy soup.

INGREDIENTS

2–3 tbsp olive oil

700 g/1 lb 9 oz ripe tomatoes, peeled, cored and halved

3 large yellow peppers, halved, cored and deseeded

3 courgettes, halved lengthways

1 small aubergine, halved lengthways

4 garlic cloves, halved

2 onions, cut into eighths

salt and pepper

pinch of dried thyme

1 litre/1¾ pints Vegetable Stock (see page 13)

125 ml/4 fl oz single cream

shredded fresh basil leaves, to garnish

NUTRITIONAL INFORMATION	
Calories	.130
Protein	.3g
Carbohydrate	.11g
Sugars	.9g
Fat	.9g
Saturates	.3g

variation

The vegetables described give the best colour combination, but red peppers work just as well. Green peppers are slightly too bitter for this soup.

cook's tip

If you do not have a food processor, you can simply chop the roasted vegetables finely by hand in Step 3. Place them in a bowl and mix thoroughly before placing in the saucepan.

1 Preheat the oven to 190°C/375°F/Gas Mark 5. Brush a large shallow baking dish with olive oil. Arrange the tomatoes, peppers, courgettes and aubergine across the base, cut-side down, in one layer. Tuck the garlic cloves and onion pieces into the gaps and drizzle the vegetables with oil. Season with salt and pepper and sprinkle with the thyme.

2 Bake the vegetables in the oven, uncovered, for 30–35 minutes, or until soft and browned around the edges. Leave to cool, then scrape out the aubergine flesh and reserve. Remove the skin from the peppers.

3 Working in batches, place the aubergine and pepper flesh with the courgettes, tomatoes, garlic and onion in a food processor and chop to the consistency of salsa or pickle. Do not purée.

4 Place the chopped vegetable mixture in a saucepan, stir in the stock and simmer over a medium heat for 20–30 minutes, or until the vegetables are tender and the flavours have blended.

5 Stir in the cream and simmer the soup over a low heat for 5 minutes, stirring occasionally, until hot. Taste and adjust the seasoning, if necessary. Ladle the soup into warmed soup bowls, garnish with basil and serve.

broccoli & stilton soup

serves 4   **prep: 15 mins**   **cook: 30 mins**

This soup looks pretty, smells wonderful and tastes absolutely fabulous – just the thing for a midweek supper, or you could serve it with crackers and cheese for a filling weekend lunch.

INGREDIENTS

25 g/1 oz butter

1 leek, chopped

1 onion, chopped

350 g/12 oz broccoli, cut into florets

1 potato, chopped

600 ml/1 pint Chicken Stock
(see page 13)

300 ml/10 fl oz milk

3 tbsp double cream

salt and pepper

140 g/5 oz Stilton cheese, crumbled

NUTRITIONAL INFORMATION

Calories	.407
Protein	.16g
Carbohydrate	.17g
Sugars	.9g
Fat	.31g
Saturates	.19g

cook's tip

Be careful not to add too much salt when seasoning the soup in Step 3 – the crumbled Stilton is likely to have made it quite salty already.

1 Melt the butter in a large saucepan. Add the leek and onion and cook over a low heat, stirring, for 5 minutes, or until softened. Reserve 2–3 broccoli florets for the garnish and stir in the remainder with the potato.

2 Pour in the stock, bring to the boil, then cover and simmer for 20 minutes, or until the vegetables are tender. Remove from the heat and leave to cool slightly. Pour the mixture into a blender or food processor and process to a smooth purée. Push the purée through a sieve with a wooden spoon into the rinsed-out pan.

3 Add the milk and cream and season to taste with salt and pepper. Reheat the soup gently. Meanwhile, blanch the reserved broccoli florets in boiling water for 30 seconds. Drain and refresh under cold running water, then slice thinly. When the soup is hot, stir in the cheese until it has just melted. Ladle the soup into warmed bowls, garnish with the broccoli florets and serve immediately.

avgolemono

⏲ **cook: 25–30 mins**   ⏱ **prep: 15 mins**   **serves 4**

The trick with this simple, classic Greek soup is not to let it boil once you have added the eggs, otherwise they will curdle into an unpalatable mess in the saucepan and spoil the texture of the soup.

NUTRITIONAL INFORMATION	
Calories 87	
Protein 4g	
Carbohydrate 12g	
Sugars 0g	
Fat 3g	
Saturates 1g	

INGREDIENTS

1.2 litres/2 pints Chicken Stock
(see page 13)

1 tbsp finely grated lemon rind

1 fresh thyme sprig

1 fresh parsley sprig

55 g/2 oz long-grain rice

salt and pepper

2 eggs

2 tbsp lemon juice

fresh thyme sprigs, to garnish

1 Pour the stock into a large saucepan, add the lemon rind, thyme and parsley and bring to the boil.

2 Add the rice, and season. Return to the boil, reduce the heat and simmer for 15–20 minutes, or until the rice is tender. Remove the saucepan from the heat and leave to cool slightly.

3 Beat the eggs with the lemon juice. Whisk in a ladleful of the hot, but not boiling stock. Whisk the egg and stock mixture into the saucepan and simmer over a very low heat, whisking constantly, until thickened. Do not let the soup boil. Taste and adjust the seasoning, if necessary. Remove and discard the thyme and parsley sprigs,

then ladle the soup into warmed bowls. Garnish with fresh thyme sprigs and serve immediately.

cook's tip

This soup is sometimes served as a sauce with meatballs. To make avgolemono for this purpose, you should omit the rice in Step 2.

meat & poultry

This chapter is packed with main-course recipes that are sure to tempt your appetite and set your taste buds tingling. There are rich, hearty stews, such as Daube of Beef (see page 54) and Louisiana Chicken (see page 104); traditional and classic dishes, such as Irish Stew (see page 67) and Chilli con Carne (see page 56); quick and simple meals, such as Beef Stroganoff (see page 63) and Chicken Cacciatore (see page 103); and exotic combinations, such as Beef with Eggs (see page 62) and Lime & Coconut Lamb (see page 73). Whether your preference is for hot and spicy, rich and luxurious or delicate and subtle flavours, you will be spoiled for choice.

Most of these dishes don't take long to prepare – one of the advantages of one-pot cooking. Some are also cooked quite quickly, while others can be left to their own devices, bubbling gently in the kitchen while you have a well-earned rest and a glass of wine before supper. Remember that most stews and casseroles taste even more flavoursome if they are allowed to cool after cooking and are reheated the next day – and you still have only one pot to wash up.

This chapter features a wonderful collection of economical, filling and tasty dishes that are ideal for midweek family suppers and Sunday lunches. Equally, you need look no further for some superb suggestions for entertaining in style – whether the sophisticated simplicity of Paprika Pork (see page 81), or the timeless elegance of Coq au Vin (see page 100).

beef in beer with herb dumplings

cook: 2 hrs 30 mins   **prep: 25 mins**   **serves 6**

NUTRITIONAL INFORMATION

Calories	.576
Protein	.47g
Carbohydrate	.46g
Sugars	.18g
Fat	.22g
Saturates	.9g

variation

Substitute other root vegetables such as chopped parsnips or turnips for the sliced carrots, if you prefer.

Serve this traditional stew with its topping of satisfying dumplings to counteract even the coldest winter weather.

INGREDIENTS

STEW	2 bay leaves
2 tbsp sunflower oil	1 tbsp chopped fresh thyme
2 large onions, thinly sliced	
8 carrots, sliced	HERB DUMPLINGS
4 tbsp plain flour	115 g/4 oz self-raising flour
salt and pepper	pinch of salt
1.25 kg/2 lb 12 oz stewing steak,	55 g/2 oz shredded suet
cut into cubes	2 tbsp chopped fresh parsley, plus
425 ml/15 fl oz stout	extra to garnish
2 tsp muscovado sugar	about 4 tbsp water

cook's tip

Dumplings can be given a little added spice by mixing in a teaspoon of mustard powder with the flour – a delicious complement to any tasty stew.

1 Preheat the oven to 160°C/325°F/Gas Mark 3. Heat the oil in a flameproof casserole. Add the onions and carrots and cook over a low heat, stirring occasionally, for 5 minutes, or until the onions are softened. Meanwhile, place the flour in a polythene bag and season with salt and pepper. Add the stewing steak to the bag, tie the top and shake well to coat. Do this in batches, if necessary.

2 Remove the vegetables from the casserole with a slotted spoon and reserve. Add the stewing steak to the casserole, in batches, and cook, stirring frequently, until browned all over. Return all the meat and the onions and carrots to the casserole and sprinkle in any remaining seasoned flour. Pour in the stout and add the sugar, bay leaves and thyme. Bring to the boil, cover and transfer to the preheated oven to bake for 1¾ hours.

3 To make the herb dumplings, sift the flour and salt into a bowl. Stir in the suet and parsley and add enough of the water to make a soft dough. Shape into small balls between the palms of your hands. Add to the casserole and return to the oven for 30 minutes. Remove and discard the bay leaves. Serve immediately, sprinkled with chopped parsley.

daube of beef

serves 6 **prep: 20 mins, plus 8 hrs marinating** **cook: 3 hrs 15 mins**

A daube is a traditional French dish, in which meat was braised in a single piece, usually in wine. Once, it was cooked in a special pot placed over an open fire. Hot charcoal could be placed in the lid, so that the stew was cooked from both ends. Nowadays, an oven is easier and the meat is usually cut into cubes.

INGREDIENTS

350 ml/12 fl oz dry white wine	1 bay leaf
2 tbsp brandy	salt
1 tbsp white wine vinegar	750 g/1 lb 10 oz beef topside, cut
4 shallots, sliced	into 2.5-cm/1-inch cubes
4 carrots, sliced	2 tbsp olive oil
1 garlic clove, finely chopped	800 g/1 lb 12 oz canned
6 black peppercorns	chopped tomatoes
4 fresh thyme sprigs	225 g/8 oz mushrooms, sliced
1 fresh rosemary sprig	strip of finely pared orange rind
2 fresh parsley sprigs, plus	55 g/2 oz Bayonne ham, cut into strips
extra to garnish	12 black olives

NUTRITIONAL INFORMATION

Calories	.319
Protein	.31g
Carbohydrate	.10g
Sugars	.9g
Fat	.12g
Saturates	.4g

variation

Bayonne ham is a dry-cured, smoked ham from the Basses-Pyrénées. If it is not available, substitute Parma ham.

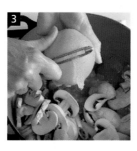

cook's tip

When you add citrus rind to a casserole, it is a good idea to grate or pare it directly into the casserole. If you prepare it too far in advance, it may dry out and lose some of its flavour.

1 Combine the wine, brandy, vinegar, shallots, carrots, garlic, peppercorns, thyme, rosemary, parsley and bay leaf and season to taste with salt. Add the beef, stirring to coat, then cover with clingfilm and leave in the refrigerator to marinate for 8 hours, or overnight.

2 Preheat the oven to 150°C/300°F/Gas Mark 2. Drain the beef, reserving the marinade, and pat dry on kitchen paper. Heat half the oil in a large, flameproof casserole. Add the beef in batches and cook over a medium heat, stirring, for 3–4 minutes, or until browned. Transfer the beef to a plate with a slotted spoon. Brown the remaining beef, adding more oil, if necessary.

3 Return all of the beef to the casserole and add the tomatoes and their juices, mushrooms and orange rind. Sieve the reserved marinade into the casserole. Bring to the boil, cover and cook in the oven for 2½ hours.

4 Remove the casserole from the oven, add the ham and olives and return it to the oven to cook for a further 30 minutes, or until the beef is very tender. Discard the orange rind and serve straight from the casserole, garnished with parsley.

chilli con carne

serves 4   **prep: 15 mins**   **cook: 30–35 mins**

This Tex-Mex favourite is often served with rice, but it is just as delicious with tortillas or thick slices of crusty bread. Buy ready-made tortillas and heat them through in a dry frying pan.

INGREDIENTS

2 tbsp sunflower oil

500 g/1 lb 2 oz fresh beef mince

1 large onion, chopped

1 garlic clove, finely chopped

1 green pepper, deseeded and diced

1 tsp chilli powder

800 g/1 lb 12 oz canned
chopped tomatoes

800 g/1 lb 12 oz canned red kidney
beans, drained and rinsed

450 ml/16 fl oz Beef Stock (see page 13)

salt

handful of fresh coriander sprigs

2 tbsp soured cream, to serve

NUTRITIONAL INFORMATION	
Calories	.437
Protein	.41g
Carbohydrate	.43g
Sugars	.16g
Fat	.13g
Saturates	.3g

variation

Substitute 1–2 finely chopped, deseeded fresh chillies for the chilli powder in Step 2. Anaheim (mild) or jalapeño (hot) are classic Tex-Mex varieties.

1 Heat the oil in a large, heavy-based saucepan or flameproof casserole. Add the beef. Cook over a medium heat, stirring frequently, for 5 minutes, or until broken up and browned.

2 Reduce the heat, add the onion, garlic and pepper and cook, stirring frequently, for 10 minutes.

3 Stir in the chilli powder, tomatoes and their juices and kidney beans. Pour in the stock and season with salt. Bring to the boil, reduce the heat and simmer, stirring frequently, for 15–20 minutes, or until the meat is tender.

4 Chop the coriander sprigs, reserving a few for a garnish, and stir into the

chilli. Adjust the seasoning, if necessary. Either serve immediately with a splash of soured cream, and coriander sprigs to garnish, or leave to cool, then store in the refrigerator overnight. Reheating it the next day makes it more flavoursome.

simple savoury mince

⏲ **cook: 1 hr**   ⏱ **prep: 10 mins**   **serves 4**

It is always worth buying the best-quality minced beef you can afford, as it will be leaner. This is not only healthier, but is also tastier and more economical, as less fat will be released during cooking.

NUTRITIONAL INFORMATION	
Calories	.286
Protein	.26g
Carbohydrate	.21g
Sugars	.9g
Fat	.12g
Saturates	.3g

INGREDIENTS

2 tbsp groundnut or sunflower oil

450 g/1 lb fresh beef mince

1 small onion, chopped

½ green pepper, deseeded and chopped

325 g/11½ oz canned sweetcorn
kernels, drained

200 g/7 oz canned tomatoes

2 tsp chopped fresh thyme

300 ml/10 fl oz Beef Stock (see page 13)
or 1 beef stock cube dissolved in
300 ml/10 fl oz boiling water

salt and pepper

fresh thyme sprigs, to garnish

1 Heat the oil in a heavy-based saucepan. Add the beef. Cook over a medium heat, stirring, for 5 minutes, or until broken up and browned. Drain off any excess fat.

2 Add the onion, pepper, sweetcorn, tomatoes and their juices and chopped thyme. Pour in the stock and bring the mixture to the boil, stirring constantly.

3 Reduce the heat, cover and simmer for 50 minutes. Season to taste with salt and pepper, garnish with fresh thyme sprigs and serve immediately.

cook's tip

You could serve this dish with plain boiled rice, but if you don't want to bother with a second pot, serve with crusty rolls and a green salad.

stifado

cook: 2 hrs 15 mins   **prep: 15 mins**   serves 6

NUTRITIONAL INFORMATION	
Calories	.270
Protein	.29g
Carbohydrate	.21g
Sugars	.7g
Fat	.8g
Saturates	.2g

variation

If you want to prepare this stew quickly, without making a stock, substitute water for the Beef Stock.

This wonderful traditional Greek stew is cooked very slowly with the result that the beef almost melts in the mouth and all the flavours mingle in a rich, thick, delicious gravy.

INGREDIENTS

450 g/1 lb tomatoes, peeled

150 ml/5 fl oz Beef Stock (see page 13)

2 tbsp olive oil

450 g/1 lb shallots, peeled

2 garlic cloves, finely chopped

700 g/1 lb 9 oz stewing steak, cut into 2.5-cm/1-inch cubes

1 fresh rosemary sprig

1 bay leaf

2 tbsp red wine vinegar

salt and pepper

450 g/1 lb potatoes, quartered

cook's tip

Fresh, uncooked rosemary sprigs and bay leaves would make an attractive garnish for this dish, but remember to remove them before eating.

1 Place the tomatoes in a blender or food processor, add the stock and process to a purée. Alternatively, push them through a sieve into a bowl with the back of a wooden spoon and mix with the stock.

2 Heat the oil in a large, heavy-based saucepan or flameproof casserole. Add the shallots and garlic and cook over a low heat, stirring occasionally, for 8 minutes, or until golden. Transfer to a plate with a slotted spoon. Add the steak to the saucepan and cook, stirring frequently, for 5–8 minutes, or until browned.

3 Return the shallots and garlic to the saucepan, add the tomato mixture, herbs and vinegar and season to taste with salt and pepper. Cover and simmer gently for 1½ hours. Add the potatoes, re-cover and simmer for a further 30 minutes. Remove and discard the rosemary and bay leaf and serve.

beef goulash

serves 4   **prep: 10 mins** ⟲   **cook: 2 hrs 15 mins** ⟲

Slow, gentle cooking is the secret to this superb goulash – which makes a warming, comforting meal on a cold evening. Rice is the ideal accompaniment to absorb the rich flavours.

INGREDIENTS

2 tbsp vegetable oil

1 large onion, chopped

1 garlic clove, crushed

750 g/1 lb 10 oz lean stewing steak

2 tbsp paprika

425 g/15 oz canned chopped tomatoes

2 tbsp tomato purée

1 large red pepper, deseeded
and chopped

175 g/6 oz mushrooms, sliced

600 ml/1 pint Beef Stock
(see page 13)

1 tbsp cornflour

1 tbsp water

salt and pepper

chopped fresh parsley, to garnish

long-grain rice and wild rice,
to serve

NUTRITIONAL INFORMATION	
Calories	386
Protein	44g
Carbohydrate	17g
Sugars	10g
Fat	16g
Saturates	5g

variation

To make a side dressing of yogurt, place 4 tablespoons of natural yogurt in a serving bowl, sprinkle with a little paprika and serve with the goulash.

cook's tip

Wild rice can be expensive, so combining it with a cheaper rice not only gives a little colour variation to this dish, but also makes it economical.

1 Heat the vegetable oil in a large, heavy-based frying pan. Add the onion and garlic and cook over a low heat for 3–4 minutes.

2 Using a sharp knife, cut the steak into chunks, add to the frying pan and cook over a high heat for 3 minutes, or until browned. Add the paprika and stir well, then add the tomatoes, tomato purée, red pepper and mushrooms. Cook for a further 2 minutes, stirring frequently. Pour in the stock. Bring to the boil, reduce the heat, cover and simmer for 1½–2 hours, or until the meat is tender.

3 Blend the cornflour and water together in a small bowl, then add to the frying pan, stirring, until thickened and smooth. Cook for 1 minute. Season to taste with salt and pepper.

4 Transfer the beef goulash to a warmed serving dish, garnish with chopped fresh parsley and serve with a mix of long-grain and wild rice.

beef with eggs

serves 4   **prep: 10 mins**   **cook: 10–15 mins**

This delicacy comes from Thailand, although similar recipes exist in the cuisines of other Asian countries. Only one saucepan is used, although the dish is cooked in individual ramekins.

INGREDIENTS

115 g/4 oz sirloin steak,
finely chopped

1 tsp grated fresh root ginger

1 tbsp Thai fish sauce

pepper

3 eggs

125 ml/4 fl oz Chicken Stock
(see page 13)

3 spring onions, finely chopped

4 whole spring onions, to garnish

NUTRITIONAL INFORMATION

Calories	.124
Protein	.12g
Carbohydrate	.1g
Sugars	.0g
Fat	.8g
Saturates	.2g

1 Combine the steak, ginger and Thai fish sauce in a bowl and season to taste with pepper.

2 Beat the eggs with the stock in a separate bowl. Stir the egg mixture into the steak mixture and add the spring onions. Whisk well to blend thoroughly.

3 Set a steamer over a saucepan of gently simmering water. Pour the steak and egg mixture into 4 ramekins and place them in the steamer. Cover and steam for 10–15 minutes, or until set. Remove from the steamer and leave to cool slightly before serving. Garnish with the whole spring onions.

cook's tip

If you are going to serve this dish as a starter, this quantity is enough for 6 people. If you don't have time to make a stock, use water instead.

beef stroganoff

⏲ **cook: 25 mins**   ⏱ **prep: 15 mins, plus 20 mins soaking**   **serves 4**

This traditional Slavic recipe makes a comforting meal on a chilly evening. Thin, delicately cooked beef and a mustard and cream sauce make this straightforward dish taste out-of-the-ordinary.

NUTRITIONAL INFORMATION

Calories	354
Protein	20g
Carbohydrate	6g
Sugars	3g
Fat	28g
Saturates	14g

INGREDIENTS

15 g/½ oz dried ceps

350 g/12 oz beef fillet

2 tbsp olive oil

115 g/4 oz shallots, sliced

175 g/6 oz chestnut mushrooms

salt and pepper

½ tsp Dijon mustard

5 tbsp double cream

fresh chives, to garnish

freshly cooked pasta, to serve

cook's tip

Ceps, also known as porcini, are widely available from large supermarkets and delicatessens. You could use other dried wild mushrooms instead, if you prefer.

1 Place the dried ceps in a bowl and cover with hot water. Leave to soak for 20 minutes. Meanwhile, cut the beef against the grain into 5-mm/¼-inch thick slices, then into 1-cm/½-inch long strips, and reserve.

2 Drain the mushrooms, reserving the soaking liquid, and chop. Sieve the soaking liquid through a fine-mesh sieve or coffee filter and reserve.

3 Heat half the oil in a large frying pan. Add the shallots and cook over a low heat, stirring occasionally, for 5 minutes, or until softened. Add the dried mushrooms, reserved soaking water and whole chestnut mushrooms and cook, stirring frequently, for 10 minutes, or until almost all of the liquid has evaporated, then transfer the mixture to a plate.

4 Heat the remaining oil in the frying pan, add the beef and cook, stirring frequently, for 4 minutes, or until browned all over. You may need to do this in batches. Return the mushroom mixture to the frying pan and season to taste with salt and pepper. Place the mustard and cream in a small bowl and stir to mix, then fold into the mixture. Heat through gently, then serve with freshly cooked pasta, garnished with chives.

sweet & sour venison stir-fry

cook: 15 mins **prep: 15 mins** serves 4

NUTRITIONAL INFORMATION	
Calories	.219
Protein	.23g
Carbohydrate	.20g
Sugars	.18g
Fat	.5g
Saturates	.1g

Venison is super-lean and low in fat, so it's the perfect choice for a healthy diet. Cooked quickly with crisp vegetables, it makes an ideal ingredient for a light, tasty stir-fry.

INGREDIENTS

350 g/12 oz lean venison steak
1 bunch of spring onions
1 red pepper
100 g/3½ oz mangetout
100 g/3½ oz baby corn cobs
1 tbsp vegetable oil
1 garlic clove, crushed
2.5-cm/1-inch piece fresh root ginger, finely chopped

3 tbsp light soy sauce, plus
extra for dipping
1 tbsp white wine vinegar
2 tbsp dry sherry
2 tsp clear honey
225 g/8 oz canned pineapple pieces
in natural juice, drained
25 g/1 oz beansprouts
freshly cooked rice, to serve

variation

For a meal-in-one, cook 225 g/8 oz of egg noodles and add to the wok in Step 4 with the beansprouts and an extra 2 tablespoons of soy sauce.

cook's tip

Wild venison has a very strong flavour, and can become tough when cooked. Buy farmed venison for this recipe, which is more tender and has a lighter flavour.

1 Trim any fat from the venison and cut into thin strips. Cut the spring onions into 2.5-cm/1-inch pieces. Halve and deseed the red pepper and cut into 2.5-cm/1-inch pieces. Trim the mangetout and baby corn.

2 Heat the vegetable oil in a preheated wok or large frying pan over a high heat. Add the venison, garlic and ginger and stir-fry for 5 minutes. Add the spring onions, red pepper, mangetout and baby corn cobs, then stir in the soy sauce, vinegar, sherry and honey. Stir-fry for a further 5 minutes.

3 Carefully stir in the pineapple pieces and beansprouts and cook for a further 1–2 minutes to heat through. Serve with freshly cooked rice and extra soy sauce for dipping.

lamb with pears

serves 4   **prep: 10 mins** ⟲   **cook: 2 hrs** ⟳

A rich and often quite fatty meat, lamb is usually partnered with sharp fruit, such as redcurrants, or tangy mint to bring out its flavour. This unusual combination is just as delicious.

INGREDIENTS

1 tbsp olive oil

1 kg/2 lb 4 oz best end-of-neck lamb cutlets, trimmed of visible fat

6 pears, peeled, cored and quartered

1 tsp ground ginger

4 potatoes, diced

4 tbsp dry cider

salt and pepper

450 g/1 lb green beans

2 tbsp snipped fresh chives, to garnish

NUTRITIONAL INFORMATION	
Calories	.504
Protein	.37g
Carbohydrate	.53g
Sugars	.27g
Fat	.17g
Saturates	.7g

cook's tip

Look for pears that are still firm even when ripe, such as Beurre Dumont, Forelle or Williams. Soft pears will begin to disintegrate during the cooking process.

1 Preheat the oven to 160°C/325°F/Gas Mark 3. Heat the olive oil in a flameproof casserole over a medium heat. Add the lamb and cook, turning frequently, for 5–10 minutes, or until browned on all sides.

2 Arrange the pear quarters on top, then sprinkle over the ginger. Cover with the potatoes. Pour in the cider and season to taste with salt and pepper. Cover and cook in the preheated oven for 1¼ hours.

3 Trim the stalk ends of the green beans. Remove the casserole from the oven and add the beans, then re-cover and return to the oven for a further 30 minutes. Taste and adjust the seasoning. Sprinkle with the chives and serve.

irish stew

cook: 2 hrs 30 mins   **prep: 10 mins**   serves 4

Nothing could be simpler, tastier or more economical than this traditional, heart-warming stew. Serve with fresh soda bread for an authentic touch – and to mop up the delicious juices.

NUTRITIONAL INFORMATION	
Calories	496
Protein	40g
Carbohydrate	55g
Sugars	16g
Fat	15g
Saturates	6g

INGREDIENTS

4 tbsp plain flour

salt and pepper

1.3 kg/3 lb middle neck of lamb,
trimmed of visible fat

3 large onions, chopped

3 carrots, sliced

450 g/1 lb potatoes, quartered

½ tsp dried thyme

850 ml/1½ pints hot Beef Stock
(see page 13)

2 tbsp chopped fresh parsley,
to garnish

cook's tip

This stew is even more substantial and flavoursome if it is served with Herb Dumplings (see page 53). Add them to the casserole 30 minutes before the end of the cooking time.

1 Preheat the oven to 160°C/325°F/Gas Mark 3. Spread the flour on a plate and season with salt and pepper. Roll the pieces of lamb in the flour to coat, shaking off any excess, and arrange in the base of a casserole.

2 Layer the onions, carrots and potatoes on top of the lamb.

3 Sprinkle in the thyme and pour in the stock, then cover and cook in the preheated oven for 2½ hours. Garnish with the chopped fresh parsley and serve straight from the casserole.

french country casserole

serves 6   **prep: 15 mins**   **cook: 2 hrs 15 mins**

*A crispy potato topping covers a dish of succulent, tender lamb,
flavoured with mint, leeks and apricots in this traditional rustic
casserole – which tastes as good as it looks.*

INGREDIENTS

2 tbsp sunflower oil	1 tbsp tomato purée
2 kg/4 lb 8 oz boneless leg of lamb, cut	1 tbsp sugar
into 2.5-cm/1-inch cubes	2 tbsp chopped fresh mint
6 leeks, sliced	115 g/4 oz dried apricots, chopped
1 tbsp plain flour	salt and pepper
150 ml/5 fl oz rosé wine	1 kg/2 lb 4 oz potatoes, sliced
300 ml/10 fl oz Chicken Stock	3 tbsp melted unsalted butter
(see page 13)	fresh mint sprigs, to garnish

NUTRITIONAL INFORMATION

Calories	720
Protein	. . . . .60g
Carbohydrate	. . . . .44g
Sugars	. . . . .15g
Fat	. . . . .33g
Saturates	. . . . .15g

variation

Use a light red wine instead of rosé
if you would prefer a slightly heavier
flavour in this country casserole.

cook's tip

It is always a good idea
to fry off meat to brown it
before adding it to a casserole.
This will ensure that it has
an appetizing colour in the
finished dish.

1 Preheat the oven
to 180°C/350°F/Gas
Mark 4. Heat the oil in a large,
flameproof casserole. Add the
lamb in batches and cook over
a medium heat, stirring, for
5–8 minutes, or until browned.
Transfer to a plate.

2 Add the sliced leeks
to the casserole and
cook, stirring occasionally, for
5 minutes, or until softened.
Sprinkle in the flour and cook,
stirring, for 1 minute. Pour in
the wine and stock and bring
to the boil, stirring. Stir in the
tomato purée, sugar, chopped
mint and apricots and season
to taste with salt and pepper.

3 Return the lamb to
the casserole and stir.
Arrange the potato slices on
top and brush with the melted
butter. Cover and bake in the
preheated oven for 1½ hours.

4 Increase the oven
temperature to 200°C/
400°F/Gas Mark 6, uncover the
casserole and bake for a further
30 minutes, or until the potato
topping is golden brown. Serve
immediately, garnished with
fresh mint sprigs.

lamb & potato moussaka

 cook: 1 hr 15 mins

 prep: 20 mins, plus 20 mins standing

serves 4

NUTRITIONAL INFORMATION	
Calories	.422
Protein	.32g
Carbohydrate	.35g
Sugars	.8g
Fat	.18g
Saturates	.8g

Minced lamb makes a very tasty and authentic moussaka –
a traditional Greek meat and vegetable pie.

variation

To ring the changes in this moussaka recipe, substitute beef mince for the lamb, and use beef-flavoured stock.

INGREDIENTS

1 large aubergine, sliced	2 tbsp water
salt and pepper	500 g/1 lb 2 oz potatoes, parboiled for
1 tbsp olive oil	10 minutes and sliced
1 onion, chopped finely	2 eggs
1 garlic clove, crushed	125 g/4½ oz low-fat soft cheese
350 g/12 oz fresh lean lamb mince	150 ml/5 fl oz low-fat natural yogurt
250 g/9 oz mushrooms, sliced	55 g/2 oz low-fat mature Cheddar
425 g/15 oz canned chopped	cheese, grated
tomatoes with herbs	fresh flat-leaved parsley sprigs,
150 ml/5 fl oz lamb stock	to garnish
2 tbsp cornflour	green salad, to serve

cook's tip

You do not have to use a meat-based stock for this moussaka – a good quality Vegetable Stock (see page 13) works just as well.

1 Preheat the oven to 190°C/375°F/Gas Mark 5. Lay the aubergine slices on a clean board and sprinkle with salt. Leave for 10 minutes, then turn the slices over and repeat. Place in a colander, rinse and drain.

2 While the aubergines are standing, heat the oil in a large saucepan. Add the onion and garlic and cook for 3–4 minutes. Add the lamb and mushrooms and cook over a medium heat for 5 minutes, or until browned. Stir in the tomatoes and stock, bring to the boil and simmer for 10 minutes. Mix the cornflour and water together to make a smooth paste, then stir into the saucepan. Cook, stirring constantly, until thickened.

3 Spoon half the mixture into an ovenproof dish. Cover with the aubergine slices, then the remaining lamb mixture. Arrange the sliced potatoes on top.

4 Beat the eggs, soft cheese and yogurt together. Season to taste with salt and pepper, then pour over the potatoes to cover.

Sprinkle over the cheese and bake in the preheated oven for 45 minutes, or until the topping is set and golden brown. Garnish with flat-leaved parsley sprigs and serve with a green salad.

moroccan lamb

serves 4   **prep: 20 mins** (L)   **cook: 1 hr 30 mins**

Slow-cooking lamb with dried fruit and spices is traditional in North Africa. Stews flavoured with dried fruits, including apricots and prunes, have now become familiar elsewhere.

INGREDIENTS

500 g/1 lb 2 oz boneless leg of lamb

1 tbsp sunflower oil

350 g/12 oz shallots, peeled
but left whole

425 ml/15 fl oz Chicken Stock (see page 13)

1 tbsp clear honey

1 tsp ground cinnamon

½ tsp ground ginger

½ tsp saffron threads, lightly crushed

¼ tsp freshly grated nutmeg

salt and pepper

grated rind and juice of 1 small orange,
plus extra rind to garnish

12 no-soak dried prunes

NUTRITIONAL INFORMATION	
Calories	.335
Protein	.28g
Carbohydrate	.26g
Sugars	.24g
Fat	.14g
Saturates	.6g

cook's tip

'No-soak' dried fruit is the same thing as dried, but moist, 'ready-to-eat' fruit, is also now available in bags in most supermarkets.

1 Cut the lamb into large cubes. Heat the oil in a flameproof casserole, add the lamb and cook over a medium heat, stirring, for 3–5 minutes, or until browned. Transfer to a plate. Add the shallots to the casserole and cook over a low heat, stirring occasionally, for 10 minutes, or until golden. Transfer them to a separate plate with a slotted spoon.

2 Pour away any excess fat from the casserole, then add the stock and bring to the boil, stirring constantly and scraping up any sediment from the base. Return the lamb to the casserole and stir in the honey, cinnamon, ginger, saffron and nutmeg. Season to taste with salt and pepper, cover and simmer for 30 minutes.

3 Return the shallots to the casserole and add the orange rind and juice. Re-cover and simmer for a further 30 minutes. Add the prunes and adjust the seasoning, if necessary. Simmer, uncovered, for a further 15 minutes. Garnish with orange rind and serve immediately.

lime & coconut lamb

cook: 10 mins   **prep: 10 mins**   **serves 4**

This Thai-style curry is so delicious and tastes so authentic that your family will think you have spent hours preparing it. Only you will know just how speedy and simple it is.

NUTRITIONAL INFORMATION	
Calories	273
Protein	25g
Carbohydrate	2g
Sugars	1g
Fat	19g
Saturates	5g

INGREDIENTS

450 g/1 lb lamb fillet
55 g/2 oz creamed coconut
300 ml/10 fl oz boiling water
2 tsp groundnut or sunflower oil
1–2 garlic cloves, finely chopped
2 tsp grated fresh root ginger
2 tbsp Thai green curry paste
grated rind and juice of 1 lime
salt and pepper
2 tbsp chopped fresh coriander, plus extra to garnish
freshly cooked rice, to serve

cook's tip

Good-quality, ready-made Thai curry pastes are available in large supermarkets and specialist Asian food stores, and add an authentic flavour to home-cooked Thai dishes.

1 Cut the lamb across the grain into strips about 4 cm/1½ inches long. Combine the creamed coconut and boiling water in a jug, stirring well to mix.

2 Heat the oil in a preheated wok or large frying pan. Add the lamb, garlic and ginger and fry over a high heat for 2–3 minutes. Stir in the curry paste and coconut mixture and add the lime rind and juice. Season to taste with salt and pepper.

3 Bring the mixture to the boil, stirring constantly, then reduce the heat and simmer for 5 minutes. Stir in the chopped coriander and serve with rice, sprinkled with extra chopped coriander.

serves 6

**prep: 20 mins,
plus 8 hrs marinating**

**cook: 1 hr 30 mins–
1 hr 45 mins**

This richly coloured, spicy dish is among the most popular lamb curries from India. It makes a filling family supper when served with a generous helping of spicy naan bread.

INGREDIENTS

225 ml/8 fl oz natural yogurt	4 cardamom pods
3 tbsp lemon juice	1 onion, finely chopped
2.5-cm/1-inch piece fresh	1 fresh green chilli, deseeded and
root ginger, grated	finely chopped
2 garlic cloves, finely chopped	2 tsp ground cumin
salt	2 tsp ground coriander
900 g/2 lb lamb fillet, cut	400 g/14 oz canned chopped tomatoes
into 2.5-cm/1-inch cubes	2 tbsp tomato purée
3 tbsp sunflower oil	150 ml/5 fl oz water
½ tsp cumin seeds	2 bay leaves, plus extra to garnish

NUTRITIONAL INFORMATION

Calories	340
Protein	. . . . .35g
Carbohydrate	. . . . .8g
Sugars	. . . . .7g
Fat	. . . . .19g
Saturates	. . . . .7g

variation

Use a red chilli instead of the green chilli if you want the dish to have a slightly sweeter flavour.

cook's tip

When you cook chopped fresh chilli in a hot frying pan, stir frequently, and keep a close eye on it. Small pieces of chilli burn easily, and will quickly turn black if left unattended.

1 Place the yogurt, lemon juice, ginger and half the garlic in a non-metallic dish and mix. Season well with salt. Add the lamb. Mix well, cover with clingfilm and leave in the refrigerator to marinate for 8 hours or overnight.

2 Heat the oil in a large, heavy-based frying pan over a high heat. Add the cumin seeds and cook, stirring constantly, for 1–2 minutes, or until they begin to pop and release their aroma. Add the cardamom pods and cook, stirring constantly, for a further 2 minutes. Add the onion, chilli and remaining garlic and cook, stirring frequently, for 5 minutes, or until the onion is softened. Stir in the ground cumin and coriander.

3 Add the lamb with the marinade and cook, stirring occasionally, for 5 minutes. Add the tomatoes and their juices, and the tomato purée, water and bay leaves. Bring to the boil, stirring, then reduce the heat, cover and simmer for 1¼–1½ hours, or until cooked through and tender. Garnish with bay leaves and serve.

lamb with mint

cook: 30 mins   **prep: 10 mins**   **serves 4**

NUTRITIONAL INFORMATION	
Calories 245	
Protein 21g	
Carbohydrate 10g	
Sugars 7g	
Fat 14g	
Saturates 4g	

variation

If you prefer, use peeled, chopped fresh tomatoes rather than canned tomatoes, but add 1 tablespoon of tomato purée with them in Step 3.

A classic combination popular in many different countries, this recipe is for a mildly spiced Indian dish of minced lamb, mixed with peas. Serve with naan bread or chapatis.

INGREDIENTS

2 tbsp sunflower oil

1 onion, chopped

1 garlic clove, finely chopped

1 tsp grated fresh root ginger

1 tsp ground coriander

½ tsp chilli powder

¼ tsp ground turmeric

pinch of salt

350 g/12 oz fresh lamb mince

200 g/7 oz canned chopped tomatoes

1 tbsp chopped fresh mint

85 g/3 oz fresh or frozen peas

2 carrots, sliced into thin batons

1 fresh green chilli, deseeded and finely chopped

1 tbsp chopped fresh coriander

fresh mint sprigs, to garnish

cook's tip

To ensure that the lamb is lean, buy boneless leg, trim off all of the visible fat and mince it yourself, using a meat mincer or food processor.

1 Heat the oil in a large, heavy-based frying pan or flameproof casserole. Add the onion and cook over a low heat, stirring occasionally, for 10 minutes, or until golden.

2 Meanwhile, place the garlic, ginger, ground coriander, chilli powder, turmeric and salt in a small bowl and mix well. Add the spice mixture to the frying pan and cook, stirring constantly, for 2 minutes. Add the lamb and cook, stirring frequently, for 8–10 minutes, or until it is broken up and browned.

3 Add the tomatoes and their juices, the mint, peas, carrots, chilli and fresh coriander. Cook, stirring constantly, for 3–5 minutes, then serve, garnished with fresh mint sprigs.

five-spice lamb

serves 4   **prep: 15 mins**   **cook: 12–15 mins**

Chinese five-spice powder, ginger and soy and hoisin sauces flavour this quick and easy aromatic stir-fry – an unusual, Eastern-style dish, which is a great idea for impressing guests.

INGREDIENTS

650 g/1 lb 7 oz lamb fillet

2 tbsp groundnut or sunflower oil

1 onion, finely chopped

1 garlic clove, finely chopped

1 red pepper, deseeded and thinly sliced

1 yellow pepper, deseeded and thinly sliced

2 tsp grated fresh root ginger

175 g/6 oz green beans, halved

1 tsp Chinese five-spice powder

1 tbsp hoisin sauce

1 tbsp dark soy sauce

4 tbsp Chinese rice wine or dry sherry

TO GARNISH

2 tbsp chopped fresh coriander

1 tbsp toasted sesame seeds

NUTRITIONAL INFORMATION	
Calories	.367
Protein	36g
Carbohydrate	.7g
Sugars	.5g
Fat	.22g
Saturates	.8g

variation

To add some spiciness, add 1–2 fresh red chillies, deseeded and chopped, with the peppers and ginger in Step 2. Serve this dish with freshly cooked rice or egg noodles.

cook's tip

Chinese five-spice powder and rice wine are available from large supermarkets and Chinese food stores. Note that the Chinese spice is different from Indian five-spice powder.

1 Cut the lamb across the grain into strips about 4 cm/1½ inches long. Heat the oil in a preheated wok or large frying pan. Add the lamb and stir-fry over a high heat for 4 minutes, or until browned all over. Transfer to a plate with a slotted spoon.

2 Add the onion, garlic, peppers and fresh root ginger to the wok and stir-fry for 3–4 minutes. Add the green beans and stir-fry for a further 2 minutes.

3 Return the lamb to the wok, then stir in the Chinese five-spice powder, hoisin sauce, soy sauce and Chinese rice wine. Cook, stirring and tossing the mixture constantly, until the lamb is tender and coated in the sauce. Serve, garnished with chopped coriander and toasted sesame seeds.

pork chops with peppers & sweetcorn

serves 4   **prep: 10 mins** (L   **cook: 45 mins** (L

If you cook this luscious and simple dish on the hob, serve it with plenty of crusty bread. If you cook it in the oven (see Cook's Tip), serve it with baked potatoes. Either way, it makes a delicious meal.

INGREDIENTS

1 tbsp sunflower oil

4 pork chops, trimmed of visible fat

1 onion, chopped

1 garlic clove, finely chopped

1 green pepper, deseeded and sliced

1 red pepper, deseeded and sliced

325 g/11½ oz canned sweetcorn kernels

1 tbsp chopped fresh parsley

salt and pepper

mashed potato, to serve

NUTRITIONAL INFORMATION

Calories	.286
Protein	.24g
Carbohydrate	.25g
Sugars	.11g
Fat	.11g
Saturates	.3g

cook's tip

This casserole can also be cooked in a preheated oven, 180°C/350°F/Gas Mark 4, for 30 minutes, or until tender. Bake some potatoes alongside as an accompaniment.

1 Heat the oil in a large, flameproof casserole. Add the pork chops in batches and cook over a medium heat, turning occasionally, for 5 minutes, or until browned. Transfer the chops to a plate with a slotted spoon.

2 Add the chopped onion to the casserole and cook, stirring occasionally, for 5 minutes, or until softened. Add the garlic and peppers and cook, stirring occasionally for a further 5 minutes. Stir in the sweetcorn kernels and their juices, the parsley and season to taste with salt and pepper.

3 Return the chops to the casserole, spooning the vegetable mixture over them. Cover and simmer for 30 minutes, or until tender. Serve immediately with mashed potato.

paprika pork

cook: 35 mins   **prep: 20 mins**   serves 4

*This is a good dish for entertaining, as it can be prepared in
advance and stored in the refrigerator for up to two days.
To serve, reheat gently, then stir in the soured cream.*

NUTRITIONAL INFORMATION	
Calories 478	
Protein 38g	
Carbohydrate 10g	
Sugars 4g	
Fat 30g	
Saturates 13g	

INGREDIENTS

675 g/1 lb 8 oz pork fillet

2 tbsp sunflower oil

25 g/1 oz butter

1 onion, chopped

1 tbsp paprika

25 g/1 oz plain flour

300 ml/10 fl oz Chicken Stock (see page
13) or 1 chicken stock cube dissolved in
300 ml/10 fl oz boiling water

4 tbsp dry sherry

115 g/4 oz mushrooms, sliced

salt and pepper

150 ml/5 fl oz soured cream

cook's tip

There are 2 kinds of paprika –
sweet and hot – but both are
much milder than cayenne
pepper. Sweet paprika is the
best choice for this recipe.

1 Cut the pork into 4-cm/
1½-inch cubes. Heat
the oil and butter in a large
saucepan. Add the pork and
cook over a medium heat,
stirring, for 5 minutes, or until
browned. Transfer to a plate
with a slotted spoon.

2 Add the chopped onion
to the saucepan and
cook, stirring occasionally, for
5 minutes, or until softened.
Stir in the paprika and flour
and cook, stirring constantly,
for 2 minutes. Gradually stir in
the stock and bring to the boil,
stirring constantly.

3 Return the pork to
the saucepan, add the
sherry and sliced mushrooms
and season to taste with salt
and pepper. Cover and simmer
gently for 20 minutes, or until
the pork is tender. Stir in the
soured cream and serve.

pot-roast pork

cook: 1 hr 30 mins   **prep: 20 mins**   **serves 4**

NUTRITIONAL INFORMATION	
Calories	.850
Protein	.41g
Carbohydrate	.12g
Sugars	.4g
Fat	.70g
Saturates	.33g

variation

Substitute 2 thinly sliced fennel bulbs for the chopped celery if you would prefer an aniseed flavour in this dish.

Beef and chicken are the most popular choices for pot-roasting, but a loin of pork works superbly well, too. This is a rich and flavoursome dish that is ideal for entertaining.

INGREDIENTS

1 tbsp sunflower oil	150 ml/5 fl oz dry cider
55 g/2 oz butter	150 ml/5 fl oz Chicken Stock
1 kg/2 lb 4 oz boned and	(see page 13) or water
rolled pork loin joint	salt and pepper
4 shallots, chopped	8 celery sticks, chopped
6 juniper berries	2 tbsp plain flour
2 fresh thyme sprigs, plus	150 ml/5 fl oz double cream
extra to garnish	freshly cooked peas, to serve

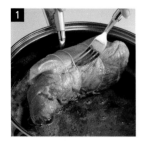

cook's tip

Remove the rind from the rolled loin of pork and trim off any visible fat, if necessary, before re-rolling and tying to prepare for cooking.

1 Heat the oil with half the butter in a heavy-based saucepan or flameproof casserole. Add the pork and cook over a medium heat, turning frequently, for 5–10 minutes, or until browned. Transfer to a plate.

2 Add the shallots to the saucepan and cook, stirring frequently, for 5 minutes, or until softened. Add the juniper berries and thyme sprigs and return the pork to the saucepan, with any juices that have collected on the plate. Pour in the cider and stock, season to taste with salt and pepper, then cover and simmer for 30 minutes. Turn the pork over and add the celery. Re-cover the pan and cook for a further 40 minutes.

3 Meanwhile, make a beurre manié by mashing the remaining butter with the flour in a small bowl. Transfer the pork and celery to a platter with a slotted spoon and keep warm. Remove and discard the juniper berries and thyme. Whisk the beurre manié, a little at a time, into the simmering cooking liquid. Cook, stirring constantly, for 2 minutes, then stir in the cream and bring to the boil. Slice the pork and spoon a little of the sauce over it. Garnish with thyme sprigs and serve immediately with the celery and freshly cooked peas. Hand the remaining sauce separately.

pork with red cabbage

serves 4   **prep: 20 mins** ⌚   **cook: 2 hrs** ⌚

The flavours of pork and red cabbage seem to have been made for each other, and here they are cooked to a melting tenderness with just a hint of fruit, sugar and spice.

INGREDIENTS

1 tbsp sunflower oil

750 g/1 lb 10 oz boned and rolled pork loin joint

1 onion, finely chopped

500 g/1 lb 2 oz red cabbage, thick stems removed and leaves shredded

2 large cooking apples, peeled, cored and sliced

3 cloves

1 tsp brown sugar

3 tbsp lemon juice, and a thinly pared strip of lemon rind

lemon wedges, to garnish

NUTRITIONAL INFORMATION

Calories	557
Protein	. . . . .38g
Carbohydrate	. . . . .16g
Sugars	. . . . .14g
Fat	. . . . .39g
Saturates	. . . . .13g

variation

For a slightly more mellow taste, you can substitute 2–3 large, firm pears, peeled and sliced, for the apples.

cook's tip

Choose a firm, glossy red cabbage for this recipe. It doesn't matter if the outer leaves are bruised, as long as the inner leaves look fresh and blemish-free.

1 Preheat the oven to 160°C/325°F/Gas Mark 3. Heat the oil in a flameproof casserole. Add the pork and cook over a medium heat, turning frequently, for 5–10 minutes, or until browned. Transfer to a plate.

2 Add the chopped onion to the casserole and cook over a low heat, stirring occasionally, for 5 minutes, or until softened. Add the cabbage, in batches, and cook, stirring, for 2 minutes. Transfer each batch (mixed with some onion) into a bowl with a slotted spoon.

3 Add the apple slices, cloves and sugar to the bowl and mix well, then place about half the mixture in the base of the casserole. Top with the pork and add the remaining cabbage mixture. Sprinkle in the lemon juice and add the strip of rind. Cover and cook in the preheated oven for 1½ hours.

4 Transfer the pork to a plate. Transfer the cabbage mixture to the plate with a slotted spoon and keep warm. Bring the cooking juices to the boil over a high heat and reduce slightly. Slice the pork and arrange on warmed serving plates, surrounded with the cabbage mixture. Spoon the cooking juices over the meat and serve with wedges of lemon.

pork stir-fry with vegetables

cook: 15 mins   **prep: 10 mins**   **serves 4**

NUTRITIONAL INFORMATION	
Calories	.216
Protein	.19g
Carbohydrate	.5g
Sugars	.3g
Fat	.12g
Saturates	.3g

This is a very simple dish which lends itself to almost any combination of vegetables that you have to hand, and makes an easy and nutritious quick lunch or evening meal.

INGREDIENTS

2 tbsp vegetable oil	1 fennel bulb, sliced
2 garlic cloves, crushed	25 g/1 oz water chestnuts, halved
1-cm/½-inch piece fresh root ginger, cut into slivers	85 g/3 oz beansprouts
	2 tbsp Chinese rice wine or dry sherry
350 g/12 oz lean pork fillet, thinly sliced	300 ml/10 fl oz pork stock
	pinch of dark brown sugar
1 carrot, cut into thin strips	1 tsp cornflour
1 red pepper, deseeded and diced	2 tsp water

variation

This stir-fry tastes just as good made with Chicken Stock (see page 13) instead of the pork stock.

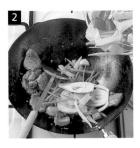

cook's tip

To make pork stock, follow the recipe for Chicken Stock on page 13, substituting 1.3 kg/3 lb of pork and pork bones for the chicken.

1 Heat the oil in a preheated wok. Add the garlic, ginger and pork and sir-fry over a high heat for 1–2 minutes, or until the meat is browned and sealed.

2 Add the carrot strips, red pepper, fennel and water chestnuts to the wok and stir-fry for 2–3 minutes, then add the beansprouts and stir-fry for 1 minute. Remove the pork and vegetables, reserve and keep warm.

3 Add the Chinese rice wine, stock and sugar to the wok. Blend the cornflour with the water to make a smooth paste and stir into the sauce. Bring to the boil, stirring constantly, until thickened and clear.

4 Return the meat and vegetables to the wok and cook for 1–2 minutes, or until heated through and coated with the sauce. Serve immediately.

pork hotpot

serves 6 **prep: 15 mins** **cook: 1 hr 20 mins**

This tasty pork and tomato hotpot requires nothing more than plenty of fresh crusty bread to mop up the delicious juices, but you could also serve it with a fresh green salad.

INGREDIENTS

85 g/3 oz plain flour

salt and pepper

1.3 kg/3 lb pork fillet, cut
into 5-mm/¼-inch slices

4 tbsp sunflower oil

2 onions, thinly sliced

2 garlic cloves

400 g/14 oz canned chopped tomatoes

350 ml/12 fl oz dry white wine

1 tbsp torn fresh basil leaves

2 tbsp chopped fresh parsley

fresh parsley sprigs, to garnish

fresh crusty bread, to serve

NUTRITIONAL INFORMATION	
Calories 500	
Protein 48g	
Carbohydrate 18g	
Sugars 5g	
Fat 23g	
Saturates 6g	

variation

Substitute 6 peeled, deseeded and chopped fresh tomatoes for the canned ones, adding them with the wine in Step 2.

1 Spread the flour on a plate and season with salt and pepper. Coat the pork slices in the flour, shaking off any excess. Heat the sunflower oil in a flameproof casserole. Add the pork slices and cook over a medium heat, turning occasionally, for 4–5 minutes, or until browned all over. Transfer the pork to a plate with a slotted spoon.

2 Add the onion slices to the casserole and cook over a low heat, stirring occasionally, for 10 minutes, or until golden brown. Finely chop the garlic, add it to the pan and cook for a further 2 minutes, then add the tomatoes, wine and basil leaves and season to taste with salt and pepper. Cook, stirring frequently, for 3 minutes.

3 Return the pork to the casserole, cover and simmer gently for 1 hour, or until the meat is tender. Snip in the parsley and serve immediately, garnished with parsley sprigs, with fresh crusty bread.

potato & sausage pan-fry

⏲ **cook: 35 mins**   ⏲ **prep: 15 mins**   **serves 4**

This dish is a meal in itself, containing both meat and potatoes cooked in a herby wine gravy. A selection of fresh vegetables may be served with the dish, if you wish.

NUTRITIONAL INFORMATION

Calories	.688
Protein	.21g
Carbohydrate	.44g
Sugars	.5g
Fat	.46g
Saturates	.19g

INGREDIENTS

675 g/1 lb 8 oz waxy potatoes,
cut into cubes

2 tbsp butter

8 large herb sausages

4 smoked bacon rashers

1 onion, quartered

1 courgette, sliced

150 ml/5 fl oz dry white wine

300 ml/10 fl oz Vegetable Stock
(see page 13)

1 tsp Worcestershire sauce

2 tbsp chopped mixed fresh herbs, plus
extra to garnish

salt and pepper

cook's tip

Use different flavours of sausage to vary the dish – there are many different varieties available, such as leek and mustard.

1 Cook the potatoes in a large saucepan of boiling water for 10 minutes, or until softened. Drain thoroughly and reserve.

2 While the potatoes are cooking, melt the butter in a large frying pan. Add the sausages and cook over a low heat for 5 minutes, turning to brown all over.

3 Add the bacon, onion, courgette and parboiled potatoes to the frying pan. Cook for a further 10 minutes, stirring constantly, and turning the sausages frequently.

4 Stir in the white wine, stock, Worcestershire sauce and chopped mixed herbs. Season to taste with salt and pepper and cook the mixture over a gentle heat for 10 minutes. Taste and adjust the seasoning, if necessary.

5 Transfer the potato and sausage pan-fry to warmed serving plates. Garnish with extra chopped herbs and serve immediately.

basque pork & beans

serves 4 **prep: 15 mins** **cook: 1 hr 30 mins**

Beans add texture and nutritional value to any casserole. Dried cannellini beans feature in many Italian, Spanish, French and Greek stews and casseroles, especially during the winter months.

INGREDIENTS

200 g/7 oz dried cannellini beans, soaked overnight in enough cold water to cover

2 tbsp olive oil, for frying

600 g/1 lb 5 oz boneless leg of pork, cut into 5-cm/2-inch chunks

1 large onion, sliced

3 large garlic cloves, crushed

400 g/14 oz canned chopped tomatoes

2 green peppers, deseeded and sliced

finely grated rind of 1 large orange

salt and pepper

finely chopped fresh parsley, to garnish

NUTRITIONAL INFORMATION	
Calories	352
Protein	. . . . .39g
Carbohydrate	. . . . .24g
Sugars	. . . . .1g
Fat	. . . . .12g
Saturates	. . . . .2g

variation

Add sliced and fried chorizo sausage for a spicier dish. Leftover beans and peppers can be used in a pasta sauce.

cook's tip

Canned, pre-cooked cannellini beans are available from some health food stores and large supermarkets. Bear in mind that the can juices may contain extra salt or sugar.

1 Preheat the oven to 180°C/350°F/Gas Mark 4. Drain the beans and place in a large saucepan with fresh water to cover. Bring to the boil and boil rapidly for 10 minutes. Reduce the heat and simmer for 20 minutes. Drain and reserve.

2 Add enough olive oil to a large, heavy-based frying pan to cover the base in a very thin layer. Add the pork, in batches, and cook over a medium heat, turning, until browned all over. Remove from the pan and reserve. Repeat with the remaining pork.

3 Add more oil to the frying pan, if necessary, then add the onion slices and cook over a low heat for 3 minutes. Stir in the garlic and cook for a further 2 minutes. Return the pork to the frying pan.

4 Add the tomatoes and bring to the boil. Reduce the heat, then stir in the pepper slices, orange rind and drained beans. Season to taste with salt and pepper, then transfer the contents of the frying pan to a large casserole. Cover the casserole and cook in the preheated oven for 45 minutes, or until the beans and pork are tender. Serve immediately, straight from the casserole, sprinkled with chopped parsley.

pork & sausage bake

cook: 1 hr 20 mins   **prep: 15 mins**   **serves 4**

NUTRITIONAL INFORMATION

Calories	575
Protein	36g
Carbohydrate	40g
Sugars	7g
Fat	31g
Saturates	11g

variation

You can use unsmoked sausages for this casserole, but you should brown them with the pork in Step 1.

This would be a lovely treat for a midweek family supper, and you can take time to relax while it's cooking. It is substantial enough to satisfy even the heartiest appetite.

INGREDIENTS

2 tbsp sunflower oil

25 g/1 oz butter

450 g/1 lb pork fillet or loin, cut into thin strips

1 large onion, chopped

1 red pepper, deseeded and sliced

1 orange pepper, deseeded and sliced

115 g/4 oz mushrooms, sliced

140 g/5 oz long-grain rice

425 ml/15 fl oz Beef Stock (see page 13)

225 g/8 oz smoked sausage, sliced

¼ tsp ground mixed spice

salt and pepper

2 tbsp chopped fresh parsley, to garnish

cook's tip

A huge variety of smoked sausages are available, from pepperoni and many types of salami to *saucisson fume aux herbes*, with a herb coating.

1 Preheat the oven to 180°C/350°F/Gas Mark 4. Heat the oil and butter in a large, flameproof casserole. Add the pork and cook over a medium heat, stirring, for 5 minutes, until browned. Transfer to a plate.

2 Add the onion and cook over a low heat, stirring occasionally, for 5 minutes, or until softened. Add the peppers and cook, stirring frequently, for a further 4–5 minutes. Add the mushrooms and cook for 1 minute, then stir in the rice. Cook for 1 minute, or until the grains are well coated, then add the stock and bring to the boil.

3 Return the pork to the casserole, add the sausage and mixed spice and season to taste with salt and pepper. Mix thoroughly, cover and cook in the preheated oven for 1 hour, or until all the liquid has been absorbed and the meat is tender. Serve immediately, garnished with chopped parsley.

spicy sausage with lentils

serves 4   **prep: 10 mins** (ᒫ   **cook: 25 mins** (ᖓ

A cross between a soup and a stew, this filling dish can be made with almost anything lurking in the storecupboard and refrigerator, so if you are short of one or two ingredients, be creative!

INGREDIENTS

1 tbsp sunflower oil

225 g/8 oz spicy sausages, sliced

115 g/4 oz rindless smoked bacon, chopped

1 onion, chopped

6 tbsp passata

425 ml/15 fl oz Beef Stock (see page 13)

600 g/1 lb 5 oz canned lentils, drained and rinsed

½ tsp paprika

2 tsp red wine vinegar

salt and pepper

fresh thyme sprigs, to garnish

NUTRITIONAL INFORMATION

Calories	.428
Protein	.23g
Carbohydrate	.23g
Sugars	.5g
Fat	.28g
Saturates	.10g

variation

You can substitute other canned pulses for the lentils, and to turn this into a fish dish, use smoked mackerel instead of the sausages.

1 Heat the oil in a large, heavy-based saucepan. Add the sausages and bacon and cook over a medium heat, stirring, for 5 minutes, or until the bacon begins to crisp. Transfer to a plate with a slotted spoon.

2 Add the chopped onion to the saucepan and cook, stirring occasionally, for 5 minutes, or until softened. Stir in the passata and add the stock and lentils. Reduce the heat, cover and simmer for 10 minutes.

3 Return the sausage slices and bacon to the saucepan, stir in the paprika and red wine vinegar and season to taste with salt and pepper. Heat the mixture through gently for a few minutes, then serve immediately, garnished with fresh thyme sprigs.

leek & sausage tortilla

⏱ **cook: 15 mins**   ⏲ **prep: 5 mins**   **serves 2**

Serve this tasty Spanish omelette-style dish with a green salad for a nourishing and tasty supper or a delicious light lunch. It is incredibly easy and quick to put together.

NUTRITIONAL INFORMATION	
Calories	.540
Protein	.33g
Carbohydrate	.10g
Sugars	.9g
Fat	.42g
Saturates	.12g

INGREDIENTS

115 g/4 oz chorizo sausage

2 tbsp olive oil

4 leeks, thinly sliced

½ red pepper, deseeded and chopped

6 eggs

salt and pepper

variation

If you like, sprinkle the cooked tortilla with 55 g/ 2 oz of grated Cheddar cheese while still in the pan and brown under a medium grill for 2 minutes.

1 Slice the sausage. Heat the oil in a large frying pan. Add the leeks and cook over a medium heat, stirring occasionally, for 5 minutes, or until softened. Add the pepper and sausage slices and cook for 5 minutes.

2 Beat the eggs in a bowl and season to taste with salt and pepper. Pour the eggs into the frying pan and cook for a few seconds. Loosen any egg that has set at the edge of the pan with a palette knife and tilt the pan to let the uncooked egg run underneath. Continue cooking until the underside has set.

3 Remove the frying pan from the heat, place an upside-down plate on top and, holding the 2 together, invert the tortilla on to the plate. Slide it back into the frying pan and cook for a further 2 minutes, until the second side has set. Slide the tortilla out of the frying pan and cut into wedges to serve.

brunswick stew

serves 6　　　　**prep: 15 mins**　　　　**cook: 1 hr 20 mins**

This traditional chicken stew is a hearty dish, which is suffused with warm, spicy undertones. Serve it with salad and wholemeal rolls to make a filling, warming winter supper.

INGREDIENTS

1.8 kg/4 lb chicken pieces	450 ml/16 fl oz Chicken Stock
salt	(see page 13)
2 tbsp paprika	1 tbsp Worcestershire sauce
2 tbsp olive oil	½ tsp Tabasco sauce
25 g/1 oz butter	1 tbsp finely chopped fresh parsley
450 g/1 lb onions, chopped	325 g/11½ oz canned sweetcorn
2 yellow peppers, deseeded	kernels, drained
and chopped	425 g/15 oz canned butter beans,
400 g/14 oz canned chopped tomatoes	drained and rinsed
225 ml/8 fl oz dry white wine	2 tbsp plain flour
	4 tbsp water
	fresh parsley sprigs, to garnish

NUTRITIONAL INFORMATION

Calories	.670
Protein	.46g
Carbohydrate	.37g
Sugars	.14g
Fat	.36g
Saturates	.11g

variation

If you don't have time to make the Chicken Stock for this dish, use water instead, which works almost as well.

1 Season the chicken pieces with salt and dust with paprika.

2 Heat the oil and butter in a flameproof casserole or large saucepan. Add the chicken pieces and cook over a medium heat, turning, for 10–15 minutes, or until golden. Transfer to a plate with a slotted spoon.

3 Add the onion and peppers to the casserole. Cook over a low heat, stirring occasionally, for 5 minutes, or until softened. Add the tomatoes, wine, stock, Worcestershire sauce, Tabasco sauce and parsley and bring to the boil, stirring. Return the chicken to the casserole, cover and simmer, stirring occasionally, for 30 minutes.

4 Add the sweetcorn and beans to the casserole, partially re-cover and simmer for a further 30 minutes. Place the flour and water in a small bowl and mix to make a paste. Stir a ladleful of the cooking liquid into the paste, then stir it into the stew. Cook, stirring frequently, for 5 minutes. Serve, garnished with parsley.

cook's tip

If you decide to substitute fresh tomatoes for canned tomatoes in a stew, add 1 tablespoon of tomato purée to the dish at the same time, to make sure that the flavour is strong enough.

provençal chicken

cook: 1 hr   **prep: 20 mins**   **serves 4**

NUTRITIONAL INFORMATION	
Calories 770	
Protein 60g	
Carbohydrate 9g	
Sugars 4g	
Fat 52g	
Saturates 13g	

variation

If you would like a little extra garlic in this dish, crush another clove into the casserole with the stock in Step 2.

This colourful dish incorporates all the wonderful flavours of southern France – olives, garlic, anchovies, tomatoes, olive oil and oregano.

INGREDIENTS

1.8 kg/4 lb chicken pieces

salt and pepper

1 garlic clove, finely chopped

3 tbsp olive oil

1 onion, finely chopped

225 g/8 oz mushrooms, halved

1 tbsp plain flour

125 ml/4 fl oz Chicken Stock

(see page 13)

175 ml/6 fl oz dry white wine

6 canned anchovy fillets, drained

3 tomatoes, peeled, deseeded and chopped

2 tsp chopped fresh oregano

6 black olives, stoned

cook's tip

Test that chicken is cooked through by piercing the thickest part with the point of a sharp knife. If the juices run clear, the chicken is ready, but if there is any trace of pink, cook for a little longer.

1 Rub the chicken pieces all over with salt, pepper and garlic. Heat the oil in a flameproof casserole. Add the chicken and cook over a medium heat, turning occasionally, for 8–10 minutes, or until golden. Add the onion, cover and cook over a low heat, stirring occasionally, for 20–25 minutes, or until cooked through and tender.

2 Transfer the chicken to a large serving plate, cover and keep warm. Add the mushrooms to the casserole and cook over a medium heat, stirring constantly, for 3 minutes. Add the flour and cook, stirring constantly, for 1 minute, then gradually stir in the stock and wine. Bring to the boil and cook, stirring, for 10 minutes, or until thickened.

3 Roughly chop 4 of the anchovies and add them to the casserole with the tomatoes, oregano and olives, then simmer for 5 minutes. Meanwhile, cut the remaining anchovies in half lengthways. Transfer the sauce and chicken to serving plates, garnish with the halved anchovies and serve immediately.

coq au vin

serves 4 **prep: 20 mins** ⏲ **cook: 1 hr 15 mins** ⏲

Traditional recipes often yield wonderfully tasty results, and this dish is no exception. Serve this perennial favourite with warm French bread or garlic bread to mop up the delicious wine-flavoured juices.

INGREDIENTS

55 g/2 oz butter	2 tbsp brandy
2 tbsp olive oil	225 ml/8 fl oz red wine
1.8 kg/4 lb chicken pieces	300 ml/10 fl oz Chicken Stock
115 g/4 oz rindless smoked bacon,	(see page 13)
cut into strips	1 bouquet garni
115 g/4 oz baby onions	salt and pepper
115 g/4 oz chestnut	2 tbsp plain flour
mushrooms, halved	bay leaves, to garnish
2 garlic cloves, finely chopped	

NUTRITIONAL INFORMATION

Calories	.966
Protein	.62g
Carbohydrate	.11g
Sugars	.2g
Fat	.69g
Saturates	.24g

variation

You can substitute a good, full-bodied white wine such as Chardonnay for the red wine, if you prefer.

cook's tip

If you like, cook the chicken in the oven instead of on the hob. Transfer it to a preheated oven, 160°C/325°F/Gas Mark 3, once the mixture has come to the boil in Step 2. Cook for 1 hour, then follow Step 3.

1 Melt half the butter with the olive oil in a large, flameproof casserole. Add the chicken and cook over a medium heat, stirring, for 8–10 minutes, or until golden brown all over. Add the bacon, onions, mushrooms and garlic.

2 Pour in the brandy and set it alight with a match or taper. When the flames have died down, add the wine, stock and bouquet garni and season to taste with salt and pepper. Bring to the boil, reduce the heat and simmer gently for 1 hour, or until the chicken pieces are cooked through and tender. Meanwhile, make a beurre manié by mashing the remaining butter with the flour in a small bowl.

3 Remove and discard the bouquet garni. Transfer the chicken to a large plate and keep warm. Stir the beurre manié into the casserole, a little at a time. Bring to the boil, return the chicken to the casserole and serve immediately, garnished with bay leaves.

chicken bonne femme

serves 4   **prep: 15 mins**   **cook: 1 hr 15 mins**

Bonne femme, meaning good woman, describes simple, rustic French dishes that are often served straight from the cooking dish. Chicken Bonne Femme is probably the most famous recipe.

INGREDIENTS

1.8 kg/4 lb oven-ready chicken

salt and pepper

55 g/2 oz unsalted butter

675 g/1 lb 8 oz baby onions

675 g/1 lb 8 oz new potatoes

6 rindless bacon rashers, diced

1 bouquet garni

NUTRITIONAL INFORMATION

Calories	1029
Protein	66g
Carbohydrate	41g
Sugars	12g
Fat	68g
Saturates	25g

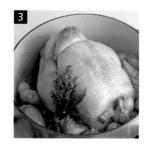

cook's tip

If you are serving this meal at a dinner party or special lunch, give the finished dish a regal look by stuffing the neck of the cooked chicken with fresh thyme and bay sprigs.

1 Preheat the oven to 180°C/350°F/Gas Mark 4. Rinse the chicken inside and out, then pat dry with kitchen paper. Season well with salt and pepper. Melt the butter in a flameproof casserole. Add the chicken and cook over a medium heat, turning frequently, for 8–10 minutes, or until golden. Transfer to a plate.

2 Add the baby onions, potatoes and bacon to the casserole and cook over a low heat, stirring occasionally, until the onions soften and the potatoes begin to colour.

3 Return the chicken to the casserole and add the bouquet garni. Cover and cook in the preheated oven for about 1 hour, or until the chicken is cooked through and tender. Remove and discard the bouquet garni. Transfer the chicken to a large serving platter, surround it with the vegetables and bacon and serve immediately.

chicken cacciatore

cook: 1 hr 20 mins   **prep: 15 mins**   serves 4

*Cacciatore refers to the Italian term 'alla cacciatora', meaning
'hunter's-style'. This recipe follows that tradition, and is a rich
and filling dish designed to give warmth and energy.*

NUTRITIONAL INFORMATION	
Calories	406
Protein	39g
Carbohydrate	10g
Sugars	7g
Fat	21g
Saturates	5g

INGREDIENTS

3 tbsp olive oil

1.8 kg/4 lb skinless chicken pieces

2 red onions, sliced

2 garlic cloves, finely chopped

400 g/14 oz canned chopped tomatoes

2 tbsp chopped fresh
flat-leaved parsley

1 tbsp sun-dried tomato purée

150 ml/5 fl oz red wine

6 fresh basil leaves

salt and pepper

fresh basil sprigs, to garnish

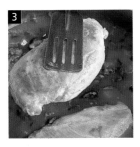

cook's tip

To make this casserole an even
more substantial meal, serve it
with freshly cooked tagliatelle
or penne, or with an Italian-
style olive and tomato salad.

1 Preheat the oven
to 160°C/325°F/Gas
Mark 3. Heat the olive oil in
a flameproof casserole. Add
the chicken and cook over
a medium heat, stirring
frequently, for 5–10 minutes,
or until golden. Transfer to
a plate with a slotted spoon.

2 Add the onions and
garlic to the casserole
and cook over a low heat,
stirring occasionally, for
10 minutes, or until golden.
Add the tomatoes and their
juices, the parsley, tomato
purée and wine, and tear in
the basil leaves. Season to
taste with salt and pepper.

3 Bring the mixture to
the boil, then return
the chicken to the casserole,
pushing it down into the
cooking liquid. Cover and cook
in the preheated oven for
1 hour, or until the chicken is
cooked through and tender.
Serve immediately, garnished
with fresh basil sprigs.

louisiana chicken

serves 4 **prep: 20 mins** ⏲ **cook: 1 hr 15 mins** ⏲

You can make this colourful American dish as mild or as spicy as you like by varying the quantity of chopped fresh chillies, or by adding a dash of hot Tabasco sauce before serving.

INGREDIENTS

5 tbsp sunflower oil	400 g/14 oz canned chopped tomatoes
4 chicken portions	300 ml/10 fl oz Chicken Stock
55 g/2 oz plain flour	(see page 13)
1 onion, chopped	salt and pepper
2 celery sticks, sliced	
1 green pepper, deseeded and chopped	TO GARNISH
2 garlic cloves, finely chopped	lamb's lettuce
2 tsp chopped fresh thyme	chopped fresh thyme
2 fresh red chillies, deseeded and finely chopped	

NUTRITIONAL INFORMATION

Calories	.573
Protein	.38g
Carbohydrate	.18g
Sugars	.6g
Fat	.40g
Saturates	.9g

variation

Substitute prawns or crayfish for the chicken. If raw, cook until they change colour in Step 1 and return to the casserole near the end to heat through.

cook's tip

The success of this dish depends on the roux (the flour and fat mixture) reaching the right stage in Step 2. It should be the colour of peanut butter. Don't try to hurry the process, or the flour will burn.

1 Heat the oil in a large, heavy-based saucepan or flameproof casserole. Add the chicken and cook over a medium heat, stirring, for 5–10 minutes, or until golden. Transfer the chicken to a plate with a slotted spoon.

2 Stir the flour into the oil and cook over a very low heat, stirring constantly, for 15 minutes, or until light golden. Do not let it burn. Immediately, add the onion, celery and green pepper and cook, stirring constantly, for 2 minutes. Add the garlic, thyme and chillies and cook, stirring, for 1 minute.

3 Stir in the tomatoes and their juices, then gradually stir in the stock.

Return the chicken pieces to the saucepan, cover and simmer for 45 minutes, or until the chicken is cooked through and tender. Season to taste with salt and pepper, transfer to warmed serving plates and serve immediately, garnished with some lettuce leaves and a sprinkling of chopped thyme.

chicken in white wine

cook: 1 hr 50 mins   **prep: 20 mins**   serves 4

NUTRITIONAL INFORMATION

Calories	894
Protein	. . . . .60g
Carbohydrate	. . . . .8g
Sugars	. . . . .2g
Fat	. . . . .63g
Saturates	. . . . .21g

Not so well known as its cousin Coq au Vin (see page 100), where chicken is cooked in red wine, this is nevertheless a popular classic and just as tasty. Serve with rice or potatoes.

INGREDIENTS

2 rindless, thick streaky bacon rashers

55 g/2 oz butter

2 tbsp olive oil

115 g/4 oz baby onions

1 garlic clove, finely chopped

1.8 kg/4 lb chicken pieces

400 ml/14 fl oz dry white wine

300 ml/10 fl oz Chicken Stock

(see page 13)

1 bouquet garni

salt and pepper

115 g/4 oz button mushrooms

25 g/1 oz plain flour

fresh mixed herbs, to garnish

variation

If you prefer, replace the bouquet garni with 1 small bunch of fresh thyme and garnish the finished dish with chopped fresh flat-leaved parsley instead of the mixed herbs.

cook's tip

If there is not much room for you to stir in Step 3, transfer the chicken to serving plates and keep warm while you whisk the beurre manié into the sauce. Spoon the sauce over the chicken to serve.

1 Preheat the oven to 160°C/325°F/Gas Mark 3. Peel the baby onions and prepare the bouquet garni. Chop the bacon. Melt half the butter with the oil in a flameproof casserole. Add the bacon and cook over a medium heat, stirring, for 5–10 minutes, or until golden brown. Transfer the bacon to a large plate. Add the onions and garlic to the casserole and cook over a low heat, stirring occasionally, for 10 minutes, or until golden. Transfer to the plate. Add the chicken and cook over a medium heat, stirring constantly, for 8–10 minutes, or until golden. Transfer to the plate.

2 Drain off any excess fat from the casserole. Stir in the wine and stock and bring to the boil, scraping any sediment off the base. Add the bouquet garni and season to taste. Return the bacon, onions and chicken to the casserole. Cover and cook in the preheated oven for 1 hour. Add the mushrooms, re-cover and cook for 15 minutes. Meanwhile, make a beurre manié by mashing the remaining butter with the flour in a small bowl.

3 Remove the casserole from the oven and set over a medium heat. Remove and discard the bouquet garni. Whisk in the beurre manié, a little at a time. Bring to the boil, stirring constantly, then serve, garnished with fresh herb sprigs.

red hot chilli chicken

cook: 40 mins   **prep: 20 mins**   serves 4

NUTRITIONAL INFORMATION	
Calories	290
Protein	36g
Carbohydrate	10g
Sugars	8g
Fat	12g
Saturates	3g

variation

If you don't have time to make the Chicken Stock, use water instead, which works almost as well.

This is a really fiery curry with a wonderfully aromatic, home-made chilli paste, for those who like it hot. You can mix the spice paste by hand with a pestle and mortar if you have to, but it is much quicker and easier to use a blender or food processor.

INGREDIENTS

1 tbsp curry paste	1 tsp ground cumin
2 fresh green chillies, chopped	1 tsp ground coriander
5 dried red chillies	½ tsp ground turmeric
2 tbsp tomato purée	400 g/14 oz canned chopped tomatoes
2 garlic cloves, chopped	150 ml/5 fl oz Chicken Stock
1 tsp chilli powder	(see page 13)
pinch of sugar	4 skinless, boneless chicken breasts
pinch of salt	1 tsp garam masala
2 tbsp groundnut or sunflower oil	
½ tsp cumin seeds	TO SERVE
1 onion, chopped	freshly cooked rice
2 curry leaves	natural yogurt

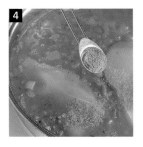

cook's tip

Indian cooks usually make their own garam masala, but it is available ready-made from supermarkets and specialist Indian food stores.

1 To make the chilli paste, place the curry paste, fresh and dried chillies, tomato purée, garlic, chilli powder and sugar in a blender or food processor and add a pinch of salt. Process into a smooth paste.

2 Heat the oil in a large, heavy-based saucepan. Add the cumin seeds and cook over a medium heat, stirring constantly, for 2 minutes, or until they begin to pop and release their aroma. Add the onion and curry leaves and cook, stirring, for 5 minutes.

3 Add the chilli paste and cook for 2 minutes, then stir in the ground cumin, coriander and turmeric and cook for a further 2 minutes.

4 Add the tomatoes and their juices and the stock. Bring to the boil, then reduce the heat and simmer for 5 minutes. Add the chicken and garam masala, cover and simmer gently for 20 minutes, or until the chicken is cooked through and tender. Serve immediately.

chicken jalfrezi

serves 4 **prep: 15 mins** **cook: 30 mins**

*This is a quick and tasty way to use leftover roast chicken. The
sauce can also be used for any cooked poultry, lamb or beef.*

INGREDIENTS

½ tsp cumin seeds	½ tsp garam masala
½ tsp coriander seeds	1 tsp red wine vinegar
1 tsp mustard oil	1 small red pepper, chopped
3 tbsp vegetable oil	125 g/4½ oz frozen broad beans
1 large onion, finely chopped	500 g/1 lb 2 oz cooked chicken,
3 garlic cloves, crushed	chopped
1 tbsp tomato purée	salt
2 tomatoes, peeled and chopped	fresh coriander sprigs, to garnish
1 tsp ground turmeric	freshly cooked rice, to serve
½ tsp chilli powder	

NUTRITIONAL INFORMATION

Calories	.270
Protein	.36g
Carbohydrate	.7g
Sugars	.3g
Fat	.11g
Saturates	.2g

variation

When in season, use fresh shelled
broad beans and if time is limited, use
ground cumin and coriander instead of
grinding the seeds yourself.

cook's tip

Chunks of lean turkey or
pork would also go well with
this combination of flavours.
With both meats, the cooking
time remains the same.

1 Grind the cumin and
coriander seeds in a
mortar with a pestle, then
reserve. Heat the mustard oil
in a large, heavy-based frying
pan over a high heat for
1 minute, or until it begins to
smoke. Add the vegetable oil,
reduce the heat and add the
onion and garlic. Cook for
10 minutes, or until golden.

2 Add the tomato purée,
chopped tomatoes,
turmeric, ground cumin and
coriander seeds, chilli powder,
garam masala and vinegar to
the frying pan. Stir the mixture
until fragrant.

3 Add the red pepper
and broad beans and
stir for a further 2 minutes, or

until the pepper is softened.
Stir in the chicken, and season
to taste with salt. Simmer
gently for 6–8 minutes, or until
the chicken is heated through
and the beans are tender.
Transfer to warmed serving
plates, garnish with coriander
sprigs and serve with freshly
cooked rice.

chicken pasanda

serves 4   **prep: 20 mins,** ⏱ **plus 2–3 hrs marinating**   **cook: 25 mins** ⏱

*This Balti dish is traditionally cooked and served in a karahi –
a pan similar in shape to a wok. If you have neither a karahi
nor a wok, use a large, heavy-based frying pan instead.*

INGREDIENTS

4 cardamom pods

6 black peppercorns

½ cinnamon stick

½ tsp cumin seeds

2 tsp garam masala

1 tsp chilli powder

1 tsp grated fresh root ginger

1 garlic clove, very finely chopped

4 tbsp thick natural yogurt

pinch of salt

675 g/1 lb 8 oz skinless, boneless

chicken, diced

5 tbsp groundnut oil

2 onions, finely chopped

3 fresh green chillies, deseeded

and chopped

2 tbsp chopped fresh coriander

125 ml/4 fl oz single cream

fresh coriander sprigs, to garnish

NUTRITIONAL INFORMATION	
Calories 426	
Protein 41g	
Carbohydrate 8g	
Sugars 7g	
Fat 26g	
Saturates 7g	

variation

If you cannot find any groundnut oil at your local food store, you can substitute sunflower oil instead.

cook's tip

When this is served in the traditional way, all the diners tear off pieces of naan bread and scoop out some of the mixture from the karahi.

1 Place the cardamom pods in a non-metallic dish with the peppercorns, cinnamon, cumin, garam masala, chilli powder, ginger, garlic, yogurt and salt. Add the chicken pieces and stir well to coat. Cover and leave to marinate in the refrigerator for 2–3 hours.

2 Heat the oil in a preheated wok or karahi. Add the onions and cook over a low heat, stirring occasionally, for 5 minutes, or until softened, then add the chicken pieces and marinade and cook over a medium heat, stirring, for 15 minutes, or until the chicken is cooked through.

3 Stir in the fresh chillies and coriander and pour in the cream. Heat through gently, but do not let it boil. Garnish with fresh coriander and serve immediately.

mexican turkey

cook: 1 hr 10 mins   **prep: 15 mins**   serves 4

NUTRITIONAL INFORMATION

Calories	355
Protein	38g
Carbohydrate	25g
Sugars	14g
Fat	13g
Saturates	3g

variation

You can also prepare this dish with 675 g/1 lb 8 oz of diced, lean beef, but you will need to allow an extra 15 minutes cooking time.

Using chocolate in savoury dishes is a Mexican tradition and, while it may sound strange, it gives the meat a very rich flavour. Mexican chocolate often has cinnamon incorporated into it, but you can use ordinary plain chocolate and ground cinnamon for this dish.

INGREDIENTS

55 g/2 oz plain flour	4 tomatoes, peeled, deseeded
salt and pepper	and chopped
4 turkey breast fillets	1 tsp chilli powder
3 tbsp corn oil	½ tsp ground cinnamon
1 onion, thinly sliced	pinch of ground cumin
1 red pepper, deseeded and sliced	25 g/1 oz plain chocolate, finely
300 ml/10 fl oz Chicken Stock	chopped or grated
(see page 13)	chopped fresh coriander, to garnish
25 g/1 oz raisins	

cook's tip

For the best flavour, choose the best quality plain chocolate you can find for this dish. It should contain a minimum of 70 per cent cocoa solids.

1 Preheat the oven to 160°C/325°F/Gas Mark 3. Spread the flour on a plate and season with salt and pepper. Coat the turkey fillets in the seasoned flour, shaking off any excess.

2 Heat the oil in a flameproof casserole. Add the turkey fillets and cook over a medium heat, turning occasionally, for 5–10 minutes, or until golden. Transfer to a plate with a slotted spoon.

3 Add the onion and red pepper to the casserole. Cook over a low heat, stirring occasionally, for 5 minutes, or until softened. Sprinkle in any remaining seasoned flour and cook, stirring constantly, for 1 minute. Gradually stir in the stock, then add the raisins, chopped tomatoes, chilli powder, cinnamon, cumin and chocolate. Season to taste with salt and pepper. Bring to the boil, stirring constantly.

4 Return the turkey to the casserole, cover and cook in the preheated oven for 50 minutes. Serve immediately, garnished with coriander.

italian turkey steaks

serves 4 **prep: 10 mins** ◔ **cook: 50 mins** ◔

This lively summer dish is simplicity itself, but tastes really wonderful and makes a surprisingly substantial main course.

INGREDIENTS

1 tbsp olive oil

4 turkey escalopes or steaks

2 red peppers

1 red onion

2 garlic cloves, finely chopped

300 ml/10 fl oz passata

150 ml/5 fl oz medium white wine

1 tbsp chopped fresh marjoram

salt and pepper

400 g/14 oz canned cannellini beans, drained and rinsed

3 tbsp fresh white breadcrumbs

fresh basil sprigs, to garnish

NUTRITIONAL INFORMATION

Calories	.264
Protein	.33g
Carbohydrate	.18g
Sugars	.11g
Fat	.5g
Saturates	.1g

variation

Soak 15 g/½ oz of dried porcini mushrooms in boiling water to cover for 20 minutes. Drain and slice, then add with the onion and peppers in Step 2.

1 Preheat the grill to medium. Heat the oil in a flameproof casserole or heavy-based frying pan. Add the turkey escalopes and cook over a medium heat for 5–10 minutes, turning occasionally, until golden. Transfer to a plate.

2 Deseed and slice the red peppers. Slice the onion, add to the frying pan with the red peppers and cook over a low heat, stirring occasionally, for 5 minutes, or until softened. Add the garlic and cook for a further 2 minutes.

3 Return the turkey to the frying pan and add the passata, wine and marjoram. Season to taste with salt and pepper. Bring to the boil, then reduce the heat, cover and simmer, stirring occasionally, for 25–30 minutes, or until the turkey is cooked through and tender.

4 Stir in the cannellini beans and simmer for a further 5 minutes. Sprinkle the breadcrumbs over the top and place under the preheated grill for 2–3 minutes, or until golden. Serve, garnished with fresh basil sprigs.

turkey in a piquant sauce

cook: 1 hr 45 mins   **prep: 20 mins**   **serves 4**

Turkey portions make an easy and economical family supper. Here they are served in a delicious tomato and pepper sauce.

NUTRITIONAL INFORMATION	
Calories	290
Protein	29g
Carbohydrate	13g
Sugars	6g
Fat	14g
Saturates	5g

INGREDIENTS

2 tbsp plain flour

salt and pepper

1 kg/2 lb 4 oz turkey pieces

25 g/1 oz butter

1 tbsp sunflower oil

2 onions, sliced

1 garlic clove, finely chopped

1 red pepper, deseeded and sliced

400 g/14 oz canned chopped tomatoes

1 sprig rosemary

150 ml/5 fl oz Chicken Stock
(see page 13)

2 tbsp chopped fresh parsley,
to garnish

variation

This recipe also works just as well with chicken pieces. Chicken is more tender than turkey, so reduce the simmering time at the end of Step 3 to 45 minutes.

1 Spread the flour on a plate and season with salt and pepper. Coat the turkey pieces in the seasoned flour, shaking off any excess.

2 Melt the butter with the oil in a flameproof casserole or large saucepan. Add the turkey and cook over a medium heat, stirring, for 5–10 minutes, or until golden.

Transfer the turkey pieces to a plate with a slotted spoon and keep warm. Add the onions, garlic and red pepper to the casserole and cook, stirring occasionally, for 5 minutes, or until softened. Sprinkle in any remaining flour and cook, stirring constantly, for 1 minute.

3 Return the turkey pieces to the casserole, then add the tomatoes and their juices, the rosemary and stock. Bring to the boil, stirring constantly, then cover and simmer for 1¼ hours, or until the turkey is cooked through and tender.

4 Transfer the turkey to a serving platter with a slotted spoon. Remove and discard the rosemary. Return the sauce to the boil and cook until reduced and thickened. Season to taste with salt and pepper and pour over the turkey. Serve immediately, garnished with parsley.

fish & seafood

The range of seafood available these days is immense, but sometimes it is difficult to know how to cook unfamiliar fish. The answer might be to put it into a pot and make a fabulous stew – Fishermen's Stew (see page 122) is incredibly easy to make and equally delicious.

This section is packed with recipes with an international flavour, from Moroccan Fish Tagine (see page 141), Thai Prawn Curry (see page 146) and the Swedish casserole Jansson's Temptation (see page 135) to Mediterranean delights, such as Swordfish with Tomatoes & Olives (see page 126). A little sophistication is also introduced with the traditional French dish, Moules Marinières (see page 143).

The following pages include ideas for preparing every kind of seafood, from prawns and tuna to monkfish and squid – and not an unhealthy chip in sight. Whether you are looking for a hot curry, a warming casserole or a traditional paella, you are bound to find a meal to suit every occasion.

cod in lemon & parsley

cook: 25 mins   **prep: 15 mins**   **serves 4**

NUTRITIONAL INFORMATION	
Calories	248
Protein	34g
Carbohydrate	9g
Sugars	7g
Fat	7g
Saturates	1g

variation

If you want to substitute another white fish for the cod, try firm steaks of whiting, halibut or haddock.

This is a very simple way to cook fish, with lovely, refreshing, Mediterranean flavours. Any firm white fish steaks or fillets are equally good at absorbing the flavours of this delicious dish.

INGREDIENTS

2 onions

1 garlic clove

2 tbsp olive oil

4 tomatoes, peeled and quartered

grated rind and juice of ½ lemon

6 tbsp dry white wine

3 tbsp chopped fresh mixed herbs, such as parsley, thyme and chives

4 cod steaks, about 175 g/6 oz each

salt and pepper

fresh thyme sprigs, to garnish

cook's tip

This is an excellent emergency dish to have on standby when you have unexpected visitors, and it tastes just as good made with frozen fish. Thaw under cold – not hot – water, or in the microwave before cooking.

1 Finely chop the onions and garlic. Heat the olive oil in a large, heavy-based frying pan. Add the onion and cook over a low heat, stirring occasionally, for 5 minutes, or until softened.

2 Add the garlic and tomatoes and cook for 3–4 minutes. Add the lemon rind and juice, white wine, chopped herbs and cod steaks, and season to taste with salt and pepper.

3 Set the heat as low as possible, then cover the frying pan and simmer gently for 15 minutes, or until the fish is cooked through and flakes easily when tested with the point of a knife. Serve immediately, garnished with fresh thyme sprigs.

fishermen's stew

serves 6   **prep: 20 mins**   **cook: 35 mins**

This richly flavoured mixture of fish and shellfish is a fabulous way to feed guests, as it is easy to prepare and needs no more accompaniment than chunks of fresh bread or crusty rolls.

INGREDIENTS

1.5 kg/3 lb 5 oz live mussels	2 tbsp chopped fresh parsley
3 tbsp olive oil	1 tbsp chopped fresh thyme
2 onions, chopped	1 tbsp fresh basil leaves, plus
3 garlic cloves, finely chopped	extra to garnish
1 red pepper, deseeded and sliced	900 g/2 lb white fish fillets,
3 carrots, chopped	cut into chunks
800 g/1 lb 12 oz canned	450 g/1 lb raw prawns
chopped tomatoes	350 ml/12 fl oz Fish Stock
125 ml/4 fl oz dry white wine	(see page 13) or water
2 tbsp tomato purée	salt and pepper
1 tbsp chopped fresh dill	

NUTRITIONAL INFORMATION

Calories	.340
Protein	.49g
Carbohydrate	.14g
Sugars	.12g
Fat	.9g
Saturates	.1g

variation

If you can't find raw prawns, use cooked ones and add them for the last 2–3 minutes of the cooking time in Step 4. They need only heat through.

cook's tip

When you buy live mussels, make sure that the shells are pristine, not cracked or broken. Always prepare them carefully, following the instructions in Steps 1 and 4.

1 Clean the mussels by scrubbing or scraping the shells and pulling off any beards. Discard any with broken shells or any that refuse to close when tapped with a knife. Rinse the mussels under cold running water.

2 Heat the oil in a flameproof casserole. Add the onions, garlic, red pepper and carrots and cook over a low heat, stirring occasionally, for 5 minutes, or until softened.

3 Add the tomatoes and their juices, the white wine, tomato purée, dill, parsley and thyme, and tear in the basil leaves. Bring to the boil, then reduce the heat and simmer for 20 minutes.

4 Add the chunks of fish, mussels, prawns and stock and season to taste with salt and pepper. Return the stew to the boil and simmer for 6–8 minutes, or until the prawns have turned pink and the mussel shells have opened. Discard any shells that remain closed. Serve immediately, garnished with basil leaves.

mediterranean fish stew

cook: 30 mins   **prep: 20 mins**   **serves 4**

NUTRITIONAL INFORMATION	
Calories 377	
Protein 51g	
Carbohydrate 13g	
Sugars 8g	
Fat 10g	
Saturates 1g	

variation

If you can't find clams, use mussels. Follow the instructions in the Cook's Tip on page 122, and make sure the shells have opened before serving.

Serve this aromatic stew in bowls or shallow soup plates, with spoons as well as forks, to ensure that everyone has plenty of the delicious tomato-and-saffron-flavoured broth.

INGREDIENTS

2 tbsp olive oil	175 ml/6 fl oz dry white wine
1 onion, sliced	350 g/12 oz red mullet fillets,
pinch of saffron threads,	cut into chunks
lightly crushed	450 g/1 lb monkfish fillet,
1 tbsp chopped fresh thyme	cut into chunks
salt and pepper	450 g/1 lb fresh clams
2 garlic cloves, finely chopped	225 g/8 oz squid rings
800 g/1 lb 12 oz canned chopped	2 tbsp fresh basil leaves, plus
tomatoes, drained	extra to garnish
2 litres/3½ pints Fish Stock	
(see page 13)	

cook's tip

Although saffron is very expensive, it has a unique flavour that is worth including in this stew and, in any case, you use only a small quantity.

1 Heat the oil in a large, flameproof casserole. Add the onion, saffron, thyme and a pinch of salt. Cook over a low heat, stirring occasionally, for 5 minutes, or until the onion has softened.

2 Add the garlic and cook for a further 2 minutes, then add the drained tomatoes and pour in the stock and wine. Season to taste with salt and pepper, bring the mixture to the boil, then reduce the heat and simmer for 15 minutes.

3 Add the chunks of mullet and monkfish and simmer for 3 minutes. Add the clams and squid and simmer for 5 minutes, or until the clam shells have opened. Tear in the basil and stir. Serve garnished with the extra basil leaves.

swordfish with tomatoes & olives

serves 4   **prep: 15 mins** ⟳   **cook: 40 mins** ⟳

Treat your family to this wonderful dish for an alfresco supper. Its flavour is very distinctive, so serve it with a side dish that won't compete – such as a straightforward green salad.

INGREDIENTS

2 tbsp olive oil

1 onion, finely chopped

1 celery stick, finely chopped

115 g/4 oz green olives, stoned

450 g/1 lb tomatoes, chopped

3 tbsp bottled capers, drained

salt and pepper

4 swordfish steaks,

about 140 g/5 oz each

fresh flat-leaved parsley sprigs,

to garnish

NUTRITIONAL INFORMATION	
Calories	.250
Protein	.26g
Carbohydrate	.5g
Sugars	.4g
Fat	.14g
Saturates	.3g

variation

Swordfish is a very firm, meaty fish, but you could substitute cod steaks, monkfish tail or even shark steaks, if you like.

1 Heat the oil in a large, heavy-based frying pan. Add the onion and celery and cook over a low heat, stirring occasionally, for 5 minutes, or until softened. Meanwhile, roughly chop half the olives. Stir the chopped and whole olives into the saucepan with

the tomatoes and capers and season to taste with salt and pepper. Bring to the boil, then reduce the heat, cover and simmer gently, stirring occasionally, for 15 minutes.

2 Add the swordfish steaks to the frying pan

and return to the boil. Cover and simmer, turning the fish once, for 20 minutes, or until the fish is cooked and the flesh flakes easily. Transfer the fish to serving plates and spoon the sauce over them. Garnish with fresh parsley sprigs and serve immediately.

griddled tuna with baby vegetables

cook: 6–8 mins

prep: 5 mins, plus 1 hr marinating

serves 4

Tuna is often served in the same way as steak – that is, slightly rare in the middle. If you prefer your fish well done, then cook the tuna for a further 1–2 minutes on each side.

NUTRITIONAL INFORMATION	
Calories	400
Protein	45g
Carbohydrate	6g
Sugars	3g
Fat	23g
Saturates	4g

INGREDIENTS

5 tbsp olive oil

2 tbsp lemon juice

1 tbsp lime juice

salt and pepper

4 tuna steaks, about 175 g/6 oz each

8 baby leeks

8 asparagus spears

8 cherry tomatoes

4 baby courgettes, halved lengthways

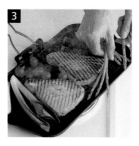

cook's tip

Depending on the size of your griddle pan, you may need to cook this dish in 2 batches. If you do not have a griddle pan, you can use a large, heavy-based frying pan.

1 Place 4 tablespoons of the oil in a shallow, non-metallic dish with the lemon juice and lime juice, and season to taste. Add the fish, turning to coat, then cover and leave to marinate in the refrigerator for 1 hour.

2 Heat a griddle pan and brush with the remaining oil. Drain the tuna steaks, season to taste with salt and pepper and add to the pan. Cook over a high heat for 3–4 minutes, then turn.

3 Add the baby leeks, asparagus, cherry tomatoes and baby courgettes. Cook for a further 3–4 minutes, then serve.

goan fish curry

serves 4   **prep: 10 mins, plus 20 mins standing**   **cook: 15 mins**

Goan cuisine is famous for seafood and vindaloo dishes, which tend to be very hot. This recipe is a mild curry, but very flavoursome.

INGREDIENTS

750 g/1 lb 10 oz monkfish fillet, cut into chunks	1 tsp cayenne pepper
1 tbsp cider vinegar	2 tsp paprika
1 tsp salt	2 tbsp cold water
1 tsp ground turmeric	2 tbsp tamarind pulp
3 tbsp vegetable oil	2 tbsp boiling water
2 garlic cloves, crushed	85 g/3 oz creamed coconut, cut into pieces
1 small onion, chopped finely	300 ml/10 fl oz warm water
2 tsp ground coriander	fresh coriander leaves, to garnish
	freshly cooked rice, to serve

NUTRITIONAL INFORMATION	
Calories	.302
Protein	.31g
Carbohydrate	.8g
Sugars	.7g
Fat	.17g
Saturates	.7g

variation

You could use any firm white fish to make this curry. Try substituting chunks of cod for the monkfish.

cook's tip

Tamarind pulp is made from the pressed pods of the tamarind tree. If you are unable to find it, substitute lemon or lime juice for the tamarind juice made in Step 4.

1 Place the fish on a plate and drizzle over the vinegar. Mix half the salt and half the turmeric together and sprinkle evenly over the monkfish. Cover and leave to stand for 20 minutes.

2 Heat the oil in a large, heavy-based frying pan and add the garlic. Brown slightly, then add the onion and cook over a low heat, stirring occasionally, for 3–4 minutes, or until soft but not browned. Add the ground coriander and stir for 1 minute.

3 Place the remaining turmeric and salt in a bowl with the cayenne pepper, paprika and cold water and stir to make a paste. Add to the frying pan and cook for 1–2 minutes. Stir the tamarind pulp and boiling water together in a bowl. When thickened and the pulp has come away from the seeds, push through a sieve with the back of a wooden spoon. Discard the seeds.

4 Add the creamed coconut, warm water and tamarind paste to the frying pan and stir until the coconut has dissolved. Add the fish and any juices on the plate and simmer gently for 4–5 minutes, or until the sauce has thickened and the fish is just tender. Serve on a bed of freshly cooked rice, garnished with fresh coriander.

spanish fish in tomato sauce

cook: 45 mins

prep: 15 mins, plus 1 hr marinating

serves 4

NUTRITIONAL INFORMATION

Calories 377
Protein 32g
Carbohydrate 10g
Sugars 5g
Fat 18g
Saturates 3g

variation

Thick cod steaks will take on the flavour of this tomato sauce just as well as the swordfish, if you prefer.

This robust and colourful Spanish sauce would go well with most white fish and you can use either fillets or steaks.

INGREDIENTS

4 tbsp lemon juice	1 tbsp plain flour
6 tbsp olive oil	225 g/8 oz tomatoes, peeled,
salt and pepper	deseeded and chopped
4 swordfish steaks,	1 tbsp tomato purée
about 175 g/6 oz each	300 ml/10 fl oz dry white wine
1 onion, finely chopped	fresh dill sprigs, to garnish
1 garlic clove, finely chopped	

cook's tip

When choosing fresh fish steaks, look for firm flesh and a fresh smell. Store the fish in the refrigerator and use it within 24 hours.

1 Preheat the oven to 180°C/350°F/Gas Mark 4. Place the lemon juice and 4 tablespoons of the olive oil in a shallow, non-metallic dish, stir well, then season to taste with salt and pepper. Add the swordfish steaks, turning to coat thoroughly, then cover with clingfilm and leave to marinate in the refrigerator for 1 hour.

2 Heat the remaining oil in a flameproof casserole. Add the onion and cook over a low heat, stirring occasionally, for 10 minutes, or until golden. Add the garlic and cook, stirring frequently, for 2 minutes. Sprinkle in the flour and cook, stirring, for 1 minute, then add the tomatoes, tomato purée and wine. Bring to the boil, stirring.

3 Add the fish to the casserole, pushing it down into the liquid. Cover and cook in the preheated oven for 20 minutes, or until cooked through and the flesh flakes easily. Serve garnished with dill sprigs.

paella del mar

serves 6   **prep: 45 mins**   **cook: 25–30 mins**

Paella is actually the name of the pan in which this famous Spanish dish is cooked – a large, heavy-based frying pan or casserole is a good substitute. This fish and shellfish version comes from Valencia.

INGREDIENTS

450 g/1 lb live mussels	175 g/6 oz monkfish fillet,
6 squid	cut into chunks
125 ml/4 fl oz olive oil	175 g/6 oz red mullet fillet,
1 Spanish onion, chopped	cut into chunks
2 garlic cloves, finely chopped	175 g/6 oz cod fillet, cut into chunks
1 red pepper, deseeded and	500 ml/18 fl oz Fish Stock (see page 13)
cut into strips	115 g/4 oz fresh or frozen green
1 green pepper, deseeded	beans, halved
and cut into strips	115 g/4 oz fresh or frozen peas
400 g/14 oz risotto rice	6 canned artichoke hearts, drained
2 tomatoes, peeled and chopped	¼ tsp saffron threads
1 tbsp tomato purée	salt and pepper
	12 raw Mediterranean or tiger prawns

NUTRITIONAL INFORMATION

Calories	623
Protein	. . . . .48g
Carbohydrate	. . . . .68g
Sugars	. . . . .7g
Fat	. . . . .19g
Saturates	. . . . .2g

variation

Any kind of firm-fleshed fish can be used in this paella. You could also experiment with other vegetables, such as chopped courgettes or asparagus.

cook's tip

Authentic paella is made with round grain Valencia rice, but this is difficult to obtain outside Spain. Risotto rice is a good substitute, or you could use long-grain rice, although this will tend to stick to the pan.

1 Clean the mussels by scrubbing or scraping the shells and pulling off any beards. Discard any with broken shells or any that refuse to close when tapped with a knife. Rinse the mussels under cold running water.

2 To prepare each squid, pull the pouch and tentacles apart, then remove the innards from the pouch. Slice the tentacles away from the head and discard the head. Rinse the pouch and tentacles under cold running water.

3 Heat the oil in a paella pan or flameproof casserole. Add the onion, garlic and peppers and cook over a medium heat, stirring, for 5 minutes, or until softened.

Add the squid and cook for 2 minutes. Add the rice and cook, stirring, until transparent and coated with oil.

4 Add the tomatoes, tomato purée and fish and cook for 3 minutes, then add the stock. Gently stir in the beans, peas, artichoke hearts and saffron and season to taste with salt and pepper.

5 Arrange the mussels around the edge of the pan and top the mixture with the prawns. Bring to the boil, reduce the heat and simmer, shaking the pan from time to time, for 15–20 minutes, or until the rice is tender. Discard any mussels that remain closed. Serve straight from the pan.

jansson's temptation

cook: 1 hr   **prep: 10 mins**   **serves 4**

NUTRITIONAL INFORMATION

Calories	373
Protein	. . . . .8g
Carbohydrate	. . . . .29g
Sugars	. . . . .8g
Fat	. . . . .26g
Saturates	. . . . .15g

variation

If fresh parsley is unavailable, then use 2–3 teaspoons of dried or freeze-dried parsley instead.

Jansson was a Swedish opera singer, as famous for his liaisons as his singing. Favoured guests visited his rooms after a performance, where he cooked for them. This was one of the meals they enjoyed.

INGREDIENTS

40 g/1½ oz butter, plus extra for greasing	1 garlic clove, finely chopped
14 anchovy fillets	1 tbsp chopped fresh parsley
450 g/1 lb potatoes, grated	pepper
2 onions, sliced	300 ml/10 fl oz single cream
	fresh parsley sprigs, to garnish

cook's tip

If you use canned anchovy fillets, you can drizzle a little of the oil over the potatoes before adding the cream in Step 2. If using salted anchovy fillets, soak them in water or milk before filleting them.

1 Preheat the oven to 200°C/400°F/Gas Mark 6. Generously grease an ovenproof dish with butter. Using a sharp knife, cut each anchovy fillet into 4 pieces.

2 Layer the grated potatoes, onion slices, garlic, parsley and anchovies in the dish, ending with a layer of potatoes, seasoning each layer with pepper. Pour half the cream over the top and dot with the butter.

3 Bake in the preheated oven for 35–40 minutes, or until the potatoes are just coloured, then pour over the remaining cream and bake for a further 20–25 minutes, or until the topping is golden and tender. Serve immediately, garnished with fresh parsley sprigs.

monkfish with onions & coriander

cook: 20 mins

prep: 15 mins, plus 1 hr marinating

serves 4

NUTRITIONAL INFORMATION	
Calories	.265
Protein	.45g
Carbohydrate	.6g
Sugars	.4g
Fat	.7g
Saturates	.1g

Monkfish is popular not just because of its fine flavour and firm texture, but also because there are none of the little bones that sometimes put people off fish. It is a meaty fish, so all you need to accompany it is a simple green salad.

INGREDIENTS

1 kg/2 lb 4 oz monkfish tail

4 tbsp lime juice

1 garlic clove, finely chopped

1 tsp ground cumin

1 tsp paprika

salt and pepper

1 Spanish onion, sliced into rings

2 fresh red chillies, deseeded and finely chopped

1 tbsp chopped fresh coriander

2 tbsp olive oil

fresh coriander leaves, to garnish

variation

Substitute green chillies for the red chillies if you would prefer a slightly more bitter spiciness in this dish.

cook's tip

Be careful not to leave the monkfish fillets to marinate for more than 1 hour, otherwise the lime juice will begin to 'cook' the flesh.

1 Remove the grey membrane that covers the monkfish tail with a sharp knife, then cut along one side of the central bone to remove the fillet of flesh. Repeat on the other side to remove the other fillet from the bone, then tie the 2 fillets together with string. Transfer the tied fillets to a shallow, non-metallic, ovenproof dish.

2 Place the lime juice, garlic, cumin and paprika in a bowl, stir to mix, and season to taste with salt and pepper. Spoon the marinade over the monkfish, cover and leave to marinate in the refrigerator for 1 hour.

3 Preheat the oven to 220°C/425°F/Gas Mark 7. Sprinkle the onion rings, chillies and the chopped coriander over the fish and drizzle with the oil. Roast in the preheated oven for 20 minutes, or until cooked through and the flesh flakes easily. Cut the fish into slices, garnish with fresh coriander leaves and serve.

cotriade

serves 4 **prep: 15 mins, plus ⏲ 10 mins standing** **cook: 45 mins ⏲**

This is a rich French stew of fish and vegetables, flavoured with saffron and fresh herbs. To serve it traditionally, ladle it over the slices of thick crusty bread, rather than serving it separately.

INGREDIENTS

large pinch of saffron threads

600 ml/1 pint hot Fish Stock (see page 13)

1 tbsp olive oil

2 tbsp butter

1 onion, sliced

2 garlic cloves, chopped

450 g/1 lb potatoes, cut into chunks

1 leek, sliced

1 small fennel bulb, thinly sliced

150 ml/5 fl oz dry white wine

1 tbsp fresh thyme leaves

2 bay leaves

4 ripe tomatoes, peeled and chopped

900 g/2 lb mixed fish fillets, such as haddock, hake and mackerel, roughly chopped

2 tbsp chopped fresh parsley

salt and pepper

crusty bread, to serve

TO GARNISH

lemon slices

fresh dill sprigs

NUTRITIONAL INFORMATION

Calories	.81
Protein	.7.4g
Carbohydrate	.4g
Sugars	.1g
Fat	.4g
Saturates	.1g

variation

Use as wide a variety of fish as possible to make this soup – such as chunks of grey and red mullet, sea bass, cod, John Dory or Dover sole, or even eels.

cook's tip

Once the fish and vegetables have been cooked, you could process the soup in a blender or food processor and sieve it to give a smooth fish soup.

1 Place the saffron in a mortar and crush with a pestle, then add it to the Fish Stock. Stir the mixture and leave to stand for at least 10 minutes.

2 Heat the olive oil and butter in a large, heavy-based saucepan or flameproof casserole. Add the onion and cook over a low heat, stirring occasionally, for 4–5 minutes, or until softened. Add the garlic, potatoes, leek and fennel. Cover and cook for a further 10–15 minutes, or until the vegetables are softened.

3 Add the white wine and simmer rapidly for 3–4 minutes, or until reduced by about half. Add the thyme, bay leaves and tomatoes and stir well. Add the saffron-infused Fish Stock. Bring to the boil, reduce the heat to low, cover and simmer for 15 minutes, or until the vegetables are tender.

4 Add the fish, return to the boil and simmer for a further 3–4 minutes, or until the fish is tender. Add the parsley and season to taste with salt and pepper. Transfer the fish and vegetables to separate warmed serving dishes with a slotted spoon and garnish with lemon slices and fresh dill sprigs. Serve with crusty bread.

moroccan fish tagine

cook: 1 hr 15 mins   **prep: 10 mins**   **serves 4**

NUTRITIONAL INFORMATION

Calories 188
Protein 17g
Carbohydrate 7g
Sugars 5g
Fat 11g
Saturates 1g

variation

You can use chopped fresh tomatoes instead of canned tomatoes if you wish, but add 1 tablespoon of tomato purée in Step 2 to give extra flavour.

A tagine is a Moroccan cooking vessel consisting of an earthenware dish with a domed lid that has a steam hole in the top.

INGREDIENTS

2 tbsp olive oil

1 large onion, finely chopped

pinch of saffron threads

½ tsp ground cinnamon

1 tsp ground coriander

½ tsp ground cumin

½ tsp ground turmeric

200 g/7 oz canned chopped tomatoes

300 ml/10 fl oz Fish Stock

(see page 13)

4 small red mullet, cleaned,

boned and heads and

tails removed

55 g/2 oz stoned green olives

1 tbsp chopped preserved lemon

3 tbsp chopped fresh coriander

salt and pepper

freshly cooked couscous, to serve

cook's tip

To preserve lemons, quarter them lengthways without cutting right through, then pack in a jar with 55 g/2 oz of sea salt per lemon. Add the juice of 1 lemon, cover with water and leave for 1 month.

1 Heat the olive oil in a flameproof casserole. Add the onion and cook gently over a very low heat, stirring occasionally, for 10 minutes, or until softened, but not coloured. Add the saffron, cinnamon, ground coriander, cumin and turmeric and cook for a further 30 seconds, stirring constantly.

2 Add the tomatoes and Fish Stock and stir well. Bring to the boil, reduce the heat, cover and simmer for 15 minutes. Uncover and simmer for 20–35 minutes, or until thickened.

3 Cut each red mullet in half, then add the fish pieces to the casserole, pushing them down into the liquid. Simmer the stew for a further 5–6 minutes, or until the fish is just cooked.

4 Carefully stir in the olives, preserved lemon and chopped coriander. Season to taste with salt and pepper and serve immediately with couscous.

mussels cooked with lager

serves 4 **prep: 25 mins** ⟳ **cook: 15 mins** ⟳

Mussels cooked in beer, tomatoes and hot Mexican spices make a sophisticated and attractive dish for a summertime dinner party, and are sure to be a talking point for your guests.

INGREDIENTS

1.5 kg/3 lb 5 oz live mussels

450 ml/16 fl oz lager

2 onions, chopped

5 garlic cloves, roughly chopped

1 fresh green chilli, such as jalapeño or serrano, deseeded and thinly sliced

175 g/6 oz fresh tomatoes, diced, or canned chopped tomatoes

2–3 tbsp chopped fresh coriander

NUTRITIONAL INFORMATION	
Calories	.163
Protein	.21g
Carbohydrate	.7g
Sugars	.6g
Fat	.3g
Saturates	.1g

cook's tip

Add the kernels of 2 corn cobs to the lager mixture in Step 2. A pinch of sugar might be required to bring out the sweetness of the corn.

1 Clean the mussels by scrubbing or scraping the shells and pulling off any beards that are attached to them. Discard any with broken shells or any that refuse to close when tapped with a knife. Rinse the mussels under cold running water.

2 Place the lager, onions, garlic, chilli slices and tomatoes in a large, heavy-based saucepan. Bring to the boil. Add the mussels, then cover and cook over a medium heat for 10 minutes, or until the shells open. Discard any that remain closed.

3 Ladle into individual bowls and serve sprinkled with fresh coriander.

moules marinières

cook: 10 mins   **prep: 25 mins**   **serves 4**

Served with plenty of fresh crusty French bread, this is a shellfish-lover's feast. The only extra treat you need to make this into a perfect meal is a glass of chilled white wine.

NUTRITIONAL INFORMATION	
Calories	185
Protein	26g
Carbohydrate	2g
Sugars	1g
Fat	3g
Saturates	1g

INGREDIENTS

2 kg/4 lb 8 oz live mussels

300 ml/10 fl oz dry white wine

6 shallots, finely chopped

1 bouquet garni

pepper

crusty bread, to serve

cook's tip

Never eat mussels that you have collected from the beach yourself, as they may have been polluted and could cause serious illness.

1 Clean the mussels by scrubbing or scraping the shells and pulling off any beards. Discard any with broken shells or any that refuse to close when tapped with a knife. Rinse the mussels under cold running water.

2 Pour the wine into a large, heavy-based saucepan, add the shallots and bouquet garni and season to taste with pepper. Bring to the boil over a medium heat. Add the mussels, cover tightly and cook, shaking the saucepan occasionally, for 5 minutes. Remove and discard the bouquet garni and any mussels that remain closed.

3 Divide the mussels between 4 soup plates with a slotted spoon. Tilt the casserole to let any sand settle, then spoon the cooking liquid over the mussels and serve immediately with bread.

provençal-style mussels

serves 4   **prep: 10 mins** ↺   **cook: 50 mins** ⏲

These delicious large mussels are served hot with a flavoursome tomato and vegetable sauce. Mop up the mouthwatering sauce with a helping of some fresh crusty bread.

INGREDIENTS

1 tbsp olive oil	2 tbsp tomato purée
1 large onion, finely chopped	1 tsp caster sugar
1 garlic clove, finely chopped	50 g/1¾ oz stoned black olives in brine,
1 small red pepper, deseeded and	drained and chopped
finely chopped	675 g/1 lb 8 oz cooked New Zealand
1 fresh rosemary sprig	mussels in their shells
2 bay leaves	1 tsp grated orange rind
400 g/14 oz canned chopped tomatoes	2 tbsp chopped fresh parsley,
150 ml/5 fl oz white wine	to garnish
salt and pepper	crusty bread, to serve
1 courgette, finely diced	

NUTRITIONAL INFORMATION

Calories	.253
Protein	.31g
Carbohydrate	.9g
Sugars	.8g
Fat	.8g
Saturates	.1g

variation

You can substitute a fresh thyme sprig for the rosemary, if you prefer, or use it in addition to the rosemary.

cook's tip

Check that none of the cooked mussels have damaged shells – discard any that are broken before steaming the remainder in Step 3.

1 Heat the olive oil in a large saucepan and cook the onion, garlic and red pepper over a low heat for 3–4 minutes, or until softened.

2 Add the rosemary sprig and bay leaves to the saucepan, then add the tomatoes and 100 ml/3½ fl oz of the wine. Season to taste with salt and pepper. Bring to the boil, reduce the heat and simmer for 15 minutes. Stir in the courgette, tomato purée, sugar and olives and simmer for a further 10 minutes.

3 Meanwhile, bring a large saucepan of water to the boil. Arrange the cooked mussels in a steamer and place over the saucepan. Sprinkle with the remaining wine and orange rind. Cover and steam until the mussels open. Discard any that remain closed.

4 Remove the mussels with a slotted spoon and arrange on a serving plate. Discard the herbs and spoon the sauce over the mussels. Garnish with parsley and serve with crusty bread.

thai prawn curry

cook: 10 mins   **prep: 15 mins**   **serves 4**

NUTRITIONAL INFORMATION	
Calories	150
Protein	11g
Carbohydrate	6g
Sugars	4g
Fat	9g
Saturates	1g

variation

Replace the fresh basil leaves with the same amount of fresh coriander leaves. If you prefer a milder curry, deseed the fresh chillies before slicing.

Thai cooking is renowned for its subtle blending of aromatic spices, and this mouthwatering curry is no exception.

INGREDIENTS

450 g/1 lb raw tiger prawns

2 tbsp groundnut oil

2 tbsp Thai green curry paste

4 kaffir lime leaves, shredded

1 lemon grass stalk, chopped

225 ml/8 fl oz coconut milk

2 tbsp Thai fish sauce

½ cucumber, deseeded and cut into batons

12 fresh basil leaves, plus extra to garnish

2 fresh green chillies, sliced

cook's tip

Three types of basil are used in Thailand: hairy (*bai mangluk*), sweet (*bai horapa*) and Thai or holy basil (*bai grapao*). They are all more strongly flavoured than Western basil.

1 Peel and devein the prawns. Heat the groundnut oil in a preheated wok or heavy-based frying pan. Add the curry paste and cook over a medium heat for 1 minute, or until it is bubbling and releases its aroma.

2 Add the prawns, lime leaves and lemon grass and stir-fry for 2 minutes, or until the prawns have turned pink.

3 Stir in the coconut milk and bring to the boil, then reduce the heat and simmer, stirring occasionally, for 5 minutes. Stir in the fish sauce, cucumber and basil. Transfer to a warmed serving dish. Scatter over the chilli slices, garnish with fresh basil leaves and serve.

sweet & sour prawns

serves 4   **prep: 10 mins**   **cook: 5 mins**

The flavours of dark soy sauce and sesame oil are perfectly complemented by tangy fresh root ginger and rich muscovado sugar in this Eastern stir-fry.

INGREDIENTS

4 spring onions, finely chopped, plus extra to garnish

2 tsp finely chopped fresh root ginger

450 g/1 lb cooked tiger prawns

1 tbsp groundnut or sunflower oil

2 tbsp dark soy sauce

2 tbsp muscovado sugar

3 tbsp rice vinegar

1 tbsp Chinese rice wine

125 ml/4 fl oz Fish or Chicken Stock (see page 13)

1 tsp cornflour

1–2 tbsp water

dash of sesame oil

shredded Chinese leaves, to serve

NUTRITIONAL INFORMATION

Calories 143

Protein 10g

Carbohydrate 16g

Sugars 8g

Fat 4g

Saturates 1g

variation

To serve with noodles, break up 225 g/ 8 oz of rice vermicelli into short lengths, heat 4 tablespoons of oil in the wok and stir-fry in batches.

cook's tip

Rather than discarding prawn heads and shells, you can use them to make a delicately flavoured shellfish stock by simmering them gently in enough water to cover.

1 Finely chop the spring onions, and peel and finely chop the fresh root ginger. Peel and devein the prawns, pat dry with kitchen paper and reserve.

2 Heat the oil in a preheated wok or large frying pan. Add the spring onions and ginger and stir-fry over a high heat for 1 minute.

Add the soy sauce, sugar, vinegar, rice wine and stock and bring to the boil.

3 Place the cornflour and water in a small bowl and mix to make a paste. Stir 1 tablespoon of the paste into the sauce and add the prawns. Cook, stirring, until slightly thickened and smooth. Sprinkle with sesame oil.

4 Make a bed of Chinese leaves on 4 serving plates and top with prawns and sauce. Garnish with shredded spring onion tassels and serve immediately.

griddled squid

⏻ **cook: 5–10 mins**　　　🕒 **prep: 15 mins**　　　　**serves 4**

NUTRITIONAL INFORMATION

Calories 137

Protein 18g

Carbohydrate 1g

Sugars 0g

Fat 7g

Saturates 1g

variation

Chop 100 g/3½ oz of thawed, peeled prawns with 1 tablespoon of chopped dill and 2 chopped shallots. Use to fill the pouches. Continue from Step 2.

This recipe works best with delicate baby squid, but if you can obtain only larger squid, slice the bodies into thick rings and cut the tentacles in half before you begin cooking.

INGREDIENTS

450 g/1 lb baby squid

2 tbsp olive oil

1 bunch of fresh parsley, finely chopped

4 garlic cloves, crushed

1 tbsp grated lemon rind

1 tbsp lemon juice

salt and pepper

fresh flat-leaved parsley sprigs, to garnish

cook's tip

If you don't want to use a griddle pan for this dish, you can also cook the squid under a preheated hot grill or on a lit barbecue, turning frequently and brushing with olive oil.

1 To prepare each squid, pull the pouch and tentacles apart, then remove the remaining innards from the pouch. Slice the tentacles away from the head and discard the head. Rinse the pouch and tentacles under cold running water.

2 Heat a griddle pan and brush with oil. Add the squid pouches and tentacles and cook over a medium heat, turning and brushing with more oil occasionally, for 5–10 minutes, or until golden brown. Divide between 4 serving plates.

3 Place the parsley, garlic and lemon rind in a small bowl and stir to mix. Sprinkle the lemon juice over the squid and season to taste with salt and pepper. Sprinkle the parsley mixture over the squid, garnish with parsley sprigs and serve warm.

shellfish chilli

cook: 45 mins

prep: 30 mins, plus 1 hr marinating

serves 4

NUTRITIONAL INFORMATION

Calories	326
Protein	33g
Carbohydrate	27g
Sugars	11g
Fat	11g
Saturates	2g

variation

If you don't have time to make the Fish Stock for this dish, you can substitute the same amount of water.

For an authentic Mexican treat, serve this seafood extravaganza with ready-made tortillas, heated through in a dry frying pan.

INGREDIENTS

115 g/4 oz raw prawns, peeled

250 g/9 oz prepared scallops, thawed if frozen

115 g/4 oz monkfish fillet, cut into chunks

1 lime, peeled and thinly sliced

1 tbsp chilli powder

1 tsp ground cumin

3 tbsp chopped fresh coriander

2 garlic cloves, finely chopped

1 fresh green chilli, deseeded and chopped

3 tbsp corn oil

1 onion, roughly chopped

1 red pepper, deseeded and roughly chopped

1 yellow pepper, deseeded and roughly chopped

¼ tsp ground cloves

pinch of ground cinnamon

pinch of cayenne pepper

salt

350 ml/12 fl oz Fish Stock (see page 13)

400 g/14 oz canned chopped tomatoes

400 g/14 oz canned red kidney beans, drained and rinsed

cook's tip

If you use any frozen seafood for this chilli, make sure that it is thoroughly thawed through before you begin cooking. For a slightly milder chilli, reduce the amount of chilli powder added in Step 2.

1 Place the prawns, scallops, monkfish chunks and lime slices in a large, non-metallic dish with ¼ teaspoon of the chilli powder, ¼ teaspoon of the ground cumin, 1 tablespoon of the chopped coriander, half the garlic, the fresh chilli and 1 tablespoon of the oil. Cover with clingfilm and leave to marinate for up to 1 hour.

2 Meanwhile, heat 1 tablespoon of the remaining oil in a flameproof casserole or large, heavy-based saucepan. Add the onion, the remaining garlic and the red and yellow peppers and cook over a low heat, stirring occasionally, for 5 minutes, or until softened. Add the remaining chilli powder, the remaining cumin, the cloves,

cinnamon and cayenne with the remaining oil, if necessary, and season to taste with salt. Cook, stirring, for 5 minutes, then gradually stir in the stock and the tomatoes and their juices. Partially cover and simmer for 25 minutes.

3 Add the beans to the tomato mixture and spoon the fish and shellfish

on top. Cover and cook for 10 minutes, or until the fish and shellfish are cooked through. Sprinkle with the remaining coriander and serve.

vegetarian

Nutritionists tell us that we should eat more vegetables, but it isn't always easy to persuade the family to eat up their greens, especially if they are sitting in an unappetizing heap on the side of the plate. This chapter provides the answer, with a spectacular collection of mouthwatering vegetable dishes, from Mediterranean-style Greek Beans (see page 156) to a delicious and unusual Winter Vegetable Cobbler (see page 167).

Beans, lentils, peppers, courgettes, aubergines, broccoli, cauliflower, onions, tomatoes and even the humble potato take a starring role, and are combined with each other for a colourful, melt-in-the-mouth medley which will satisfy even the hungriest appetite. If you are in the mood for something hot, try Vegetable Chilli (see page 161), Yellow Curry (see page 164) or Spiced Cashew Nut Curry (see page 165). If you are looking for something a little more comforting, Cauliflower Bake (see page 168) or Pepper & Mushroom Hash (see page 157) will fit the bill perfectly.

A vegetarian main course is an easy way to ring the changes in the weekly menu, and nut- or pulse-based dishes can be just as nutritious as a meat or fish dish. Whatever your favourite vegetable, there will be something in this section to tempt even the keenest meat-eater to try something a little different.

greek beans

serves 4   **prep: 5 mins**   **cook: 1 hr 5 mins**

This dish contains many typical Greek flavours, such as lemon and garlic, for a really flavoursome recipe. The fresh oregano and black olives give it a real taste of the Mediterranean.

INGREDIENTS

400 g/14 oz canned haricot
beans, drained and rinsed
1 tbsp olive oil
3 garlic cloves, crushed
425 ml/15 fl oz Vegetable Stock
(see page 13)
1 bay leaf
2 fresh oregano sprigs
1 tbsp tomato purée
juice of 1 lemon
1 small red onion, chopped
25 g/1 oz stoned black olives, halved
salt and pepper

NUTRITIONAL INFORMATION

Calories	.115
Protein	.6g
Carbohydrate	.15g
Sugars	.4g
Fat	.4g
Saturates	.0.6g

cook's tip

You can substitute other canned beans for the haricot beans – try cannellini or black-eyed beans or chickpeas. Drain and rinse them before use, because canned beans often have sugar or salt added.

1 Place the haricot beans in a large, flameproof casserole dish, add the olive oil and garlic and cook over a low heat, stirring occasionally, for 4–5 minutes.

2 Add the stock, bay leaf, oregano, tomato purée, lemon juice and red onion and stir to mix. Cover and simmer for 1 hour, or until the sauce has thickened.

3 Stir in the black olives, then season to taste with salt and pepper. This dish is delicious served either warm or cold.

pepper & mushroom hash

 cook: 30 mins prep: 10 mins serves 4

This quick and easy-to-prepare one-pan dish is ideal for an evening snack. Packed with colour and flavour, it is an extremely versatile recipe – you can add whichever vegetables you have to hand.

NUTRITIONAL INFORMATION	
Calories 182	
Protein 5g	
Carbohydrate 34g	
Sugars 6g	
Fat 4g	
Saturates 0.5g	

INGREDIENTS

675 g/1 lb 8 oz potatoes, cut into cubes

salt and pepper

1 tbsp olive oil

2 garlic cloves, crushed

1 green pepper, deseeded
and cut into cubes

1 yellow pepper, deseeded
and cut into cubes

3 tomatoes, diced

75 g/2¾ oz button mushrooms, halved

1 tbsp Worcestershire sauce

2 tbsp chopped fresh basil

fresh basil leaves, to garnish

crusty bread, to serve

cook's tip

Most brands of Worcestershire sauce contain anchovies, so if you are a vegetarian, check the label to make sure you choose a vegetarian variety.

1 Cook the potato cubes in a large saucepan of lightly salted boiling water for 7–8 minutes. Drain well and reserve.

2 Heat the oil in a large, heavy-based frying pan. Add the potato cubes and cook over a medium heat, stirring, for 8–10 minutes, or until browned.

3 Add the garlic and pepper cubes and cook, stirring frequently, for 2–3 minutes. Add the tomatoes and mushrooms and cook, stirring frequently, for 5–6 minutes.

4 Stir in the Worcestershire sauce and basil and season to taste with salt and pepper. Transfer to a warmed serving dish, garnish with basil leaves and serve with crusty bread.

sweet & sour vegetables

serves 4 **prep: 15 mins, plus 30 mins standing** ⏲ **cook: 30 mins** ⏲

This is a dish of Persian origin – not Chinese, as it sounds. Plump diced aubergines are fried and mixed with tomatoes, mint, sugar and vinegar to give a unique combination of flavours.

INGREDIENTS

2 large aubergines	3 tbsp chopped fresh mint
salt and pepper	150 ml/5 fl oz Vegetable Stock
6 tbsp olive oil	(see page 13)
4 garlic cloves, crushed	4 tsp brown sugar
1 onion, cut into eighths	2 tbsp red wine vinegar
4 large tomatoes, deseeded	1 tsp chilli flakes
and chopped	fresh mint sprigs, to garnish

NUTRITIONAL INFORMATION

Calories	.218
Protein	.3g
Carbohydrate	.14g
Sugars	.12g
Fat	.17g
Saturates	.3g

variation

Substitute 1 teaspoon of chopped fresh red chilli for the chilli flakes to give the dish a slightly milder flavour.

cook's tip

Choose firm, glossy aubergines for this dish. Large aubergines benefit from salting to extract their juices – small aubergines are less bitter, and can often be cooked without salting.

1 Cut the aubergines into cubes. Place them in a colander, sprinkle with plenty of salt and leave to stand for 30 minutes to remove all the bitter juices. Rinse thoroughly under cold running water and pat dry with kitchen paper.

2 Heat the olive oil in a large, heavy-based frying pan. Add the aubergine and cook over a medium heat, stirring, for 1–2 minutes, or until beginning to colour. Stir in the garlic and onion wedges and cook, stirring constantly, for a further 2–3 minutes.

3 Stir in the tomatoes, mint and stock. Reduce the heat, cover and simmer for 15–20 minutes, or until the aubergine is tender.

4 Add the sugar, vinegar and chilli flakes. Season to taste with salt and pepper and cook for a further 2–3 minutes, stirring.

5 Transfer to a warmed serving dish, garnish with fresh mint sprigs and serve immediately.

vegetable chilli

cook: 1 hr 20 mins **prep: 10 mins** **serves 4**

NUTRITIONAL INFORMATION

Calories	.213
Protein	.12g
Carbohydrate	.21g
Sugars	.11g
Fat	.10g
Saturates	.5g

variation

If you prefer a hotter dish, stir in a little extra chilli powder when you adjust the seasoning at the end of Step 4.

This is a hearty and flavoursome dish that works well served on its own, and is delicious spooned over cooked rice or baked potatoes to make a more substantial meal.

INGREDIENTS

1 aubergine, cut into 2.5-cm/1-inch slices

1 tbsp olive oil, plus extra for brushing

1 large red or yellow onion, finely chopped

2 red or yellow peppers, deseeded and finely chopped

3–4 garlic cloves, finely chopped or crushed

800 g/1 lb 12 oz canned chopped tomatoes

1 tbsp mild chilli powder

½ tsp ground cumin

½ tsp dried oregano

salt and pepper

2 small courgettes, quartered lengthways and sliced

400 g/14 oz canned kidney beans, drained and rinsed

450 ml/16 fl oz water

1 tbsp tomato purée

6 spring onions, finely chopped

115 g/4 oz Cheddar cheese, grated

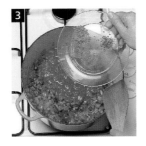

cook's tip

If you would prefer to leave the purple aubergine skin out of this chilli, you can peel the aubergine before cutting it into slices.

1 Brush the aubergine slices on one side with olive oil. Heat half the oil in a large, heavy-based frying pan. Add the aubergine slices, oiled-side up, and cook over a medium heat for 5–6 minutes, or until browned on one side. Turn the slices over, cook on the other side until browned and transfer to a plate. Cut into bite-sized pieces.

2 Heat the remaining oil in a large saucepan over a medium heat. Add the chopped onion and peppers to the saucepan and cook, stirring occasionally, for 3–4 minutes, or until the onion is just softened, but not browned. Add the garlic and cook for a further 2–3 minutes, or until the onion just begins to colour.

3 Add the tomatoes, chilli powder, cumin and oregano. Season to taste with salt and pepper. Bring just to the boil, reduce the heat, cover and simmer gently for 15 minutes.

4 Add the sliced courgettes, aubergine pieces and kidney beans. Stir in the water and tomato purée.

Return to the boil, then cover the saucepan and simmer for a further 45 minutes, or until the vegetables are tender. Taste and adjust the seasoning, if necessary.

5 Ladle into warmed bowls and top with spring onions and cheese.

vegetable curry

serves 4 **prep: 10 mins** **cook: 45 mins**

*This colourful and interesting mixture of vegetables, cooked in a
spicy sauce, is excellent served with rice and naan bread.*

INGREDIENTS

1 aubergine	2 tsp ground coriander
225 g/8 oz turnips	1 tbsp mild or medium curry powder
350 g/12 oz new potatoes	450 ml/16 fl oz Vegetable Stock
225 g/8 oz cauliflower	(see page 13)
225 g/8 oz button mushrooms	400 g/14 oz canned chopped tomatoes
1 large onion	salt
3 carrots	1 green pepper, deseeded and sliced
6 tbsp ghee	1 tbsp cornflour
2 garlic cloves, crushed	150 ml/5 fl oz coconut milk
4 tsp finely chopped fresh root ginger	2–3 tbsp ground almonds
1–2 fresh green chillies, deseeded	fresh coriander sprigs, to garnish
and chopped	freshly cooked rice, to serve
1 tbsp paprika	

NUTRITIONAL INFORMATION

Calories	.421
Protein	.12g
Carbohydrate	.42g
Sugars	.20g
Fat	.24g
Saturates	.3g

variation

You can use vegetable oil instead
of the ghee, and substitute peeled
swede for the turnip, if you prefer.

cook's tip

Ghee is clarified butter,
which contains no milk solids.
It can be heated to much
higher temperatures than
ordinary butter. It is available
from Indian food stores and
large supermarkets.

1 Cut the aubergine,
turnips and potatoes
into 1-cm/½-inch cubes. Divide
the cauliflower into small
florets. Leave the button
mushrooms whole or slice
them thickly, if preferred. Slice
the onion and carrots.

2 Heat the ghee in a
large, heavy-based
saucepan. Add the onion,
turnip, potato and cauliflower
and cook over a low heat,
stirring frequently, for
3 minutes. Add the garlic,
ginger, chillies, paprika,
ground coriander and curry
powder and cook, stirring,
for 1 minute.

3 Add the stock,
tomatoes, aubergine
and mushrooms and season
to taste with salt. Cover and
simmer, stirring occasionally,
for 30 minutes, or until tender.
Add the green pepper and
carrots, cover and cook for
a further 5 minutes.

4 Place the cornflour and
coconut milk in a bowl,
mix into a smooth paste and
stir into the vegetable mixture.
Add the ground almonds and
simmer, stirring constantly, for
2 minutes. Taste and adjust the
seasoning, if necessary. Transfer
to warmed serving plates,
garnish with coriander sprigs
and serve immediately with
freshly cooked rice.

yellow curry

serves 4 **prep: 10 mins** **cook: 15 mins**

Potatoes are not highly regarded in Thai cooking because rice is the traditional staple food, but this dish is a tasty exception.

INGREDIENTS

2 garlic cloves, finely chopped

3-cm/1¼-inch piece galangal, finely chopped

1 lemon grass stalk, finely chopped

1 tsp coriander seeds

3 tbsp vegetable oil

2 tsp Thai red curry paste

½ tsp ground turmeric

200 ml/7 fl oz coconut milk

250 g/9 oz potatoes, cut into cubes

100 ml/3½ fl oz Vegetable Stock (see page 13)

200 g/7 oz fresh young spinach leaves

1 small onion, thinly sliced into rings

NUTRITIONAL INFORMATION

Calories 160

Protein 3g

Carbohydrate 15g

Sugars 4g

Fat 10g

Saturates 1g

cook's tip

Choose a firm, waxy potato for this dish, one that will keep its shape during cooking, in preference to a floury variety that will break up easily.

1 Place the garlic, galangal, lemon grass and coriander seeds into a mortar and crush with a pestle to make a smooth paste.

2 Heat 2 tablespoons of the oil in a large, heavy-based frying pan or preheated wok. Stir in the fresh garlic and spice paste and stir-fry over a high heat for 30 seconds, then stir in the curry paste and turmeric, add the coconut milk and bring to the boil.

3 Add the potatoes and stock. Return to the boil, then reduce the heat and simmer, uncovered, for 10–12 minutes, or until the potatoes are almost tender.

4 Stir in the spinach and simmer until the leaves have wilted.

5 Heat the remaining oil in a separate frying pan, add the onion and cook until crisp and golden brown. Place on top of the curry just before serving.

spiced cashew nut curry

🕒 **cook: 25 mins**

🕛 **prep: 15 mins, plus 8 hrs soaking**

serves 4

This unusual vegetarian dish is best served as a side dish with other curries and with rice to soak up the wonderfully rich, spiced juices.

NUTRITIONAL INFORMATION	
Calories	.455
Protein	.13g
Carbohydrate	.16g
Sugars	.6g
Fat	.39g
Saturates	.11g

INGREDIENTS

250 g/9 oz unsalted cashew nuts

1 small fresh green chilli

1 tsp coriander seeds

1 tsp cumin seeds

2 cardamom pods, crushed

1 tbsp sunflower oil

1 onion, thinly sliced

1 garlic clove, crushed

1 cinnamon stick

½ tsp ground turmeric

4 tbsp coconut cream

300 ml/10 fl oz hot Vegetable Stock (see page 13)

3 kaffir lime leaves, finely shredded

freshly cooked jasmine rice, to serve

cook's tip

All spices give the best flavour when freshly crushed, but if you prefer, you can use ground spices instead of placing them in a mortar and crushing with a pestle.

1 Soak the cashew nuts in cold water for 8 hours, or overnight, then drain well. Deseed and chop the chilli. Place the coriander seeds, cumin seeds and cardamom pods in a mortar and crush with a pestle.

2 Heat the oil in a heavy-based frying pan and stir-fry the onion and garlic over a medium heat for 2–3 minutes, or until softened, but not browned. Add the chilli, crushed spices, cinnamon stick and turmeric and stir-fry for a further 1 minute.

3 Add the coconut cream and the hot Vegetable Stock to the frying pan. Bring to the boil, then add the cashew nuts and lime leaves. Reduce the heat, cover and simmer for 20 minutes. Serve hot with freshly cooked jasmine rice.

winter vegetable cobbler

cook: 40 mins   **prep: 20 mins**   **serves 4**

NUTRITIONAL INFORMATION

Calories 734

Protein 27g

Carbohydrate 96g

Sugars 22g

Fat 30g

Saturates 16g

variation

Substitute broccoli florets for the cauliflower, or chopped turnips for the swede, if you prefer.

Seasonal fresh vegetables are cooked with lentils, then topped with a ring of fresh cheese scones to make this tasty cobbler.

INGREDIENTS

1 tbsp olive oil

1 garlic clove, crushed

8 small onions, halved

2 celery sticks, sliced

225 g/8 oz swede, chopped

2 carrots, sliced

½ small cauliflower, broken into florets

225 g/8 oz mushrooms, sliced

400 g/14 oz canned chopped tomatoes

55 g/2 oz red split lentils, rinsed

2 tbsp cornflour

3–4 tbsp water

300 ml/10 fl oz Vegetable Stock

(see page 13)

2 tsp Tabasco sauce

2 tsp chopped fresh oregano

fresh oregano sprigs, to garnish

TOPPING

225 g/8 oz self-raising flour

pinch of salt

4 tbsp butter

115 g/4 oz mature Cheddar cheese, grated

2 tsp chopped fresh oregano

1 egg, lightly beaten

150 ml/5 fl oz milk

plain flour, for dusting

cook's tip

Use a scone cutter to cut out the dough rounds, to give the edges a decorative shape. When you arrange the scones around the dish, make sure that you overlap them slightly.

1 Preheat the oven to 180°C/350°F/Gas Mark 4. Heat the oil in a large frying pan and cook the garlic and onions over a low heat for 5 minutes. Add the celery, swede, carrots and cauliflower and cook for 2–3 minutes.

2 Add the mushrooms, tomatoes and lentils. Place the cornflour and water in a bowl and mix to make a smooth paste. Stir into the frying pan with the stock, Tabasco and oregano. Transfer to an ovenproof dish, cover and bake in the preheated oven for 20 minutes.

3 To make the topping, sift the flour and salt into a bowl. Add the butter and rub it in, then stir in most of the cheese and oregano. Beat the egg with the milk in a small bowl and add enough to the dry ingredients to make a soft dough. Knead, then roll out on a lightly floured work surface to 1-cm/½-inch thick. Cut into 5-cm/2-inch rounds.

4 Remove the dish from the oven and increase the temperature to 200°C/ 400°F/Gas Mark 6. Arrange the dough rounds around the edge of the dish, brush with the remaining egg and milk mixture and sprinkle with the reserved cheese. Cook for a further 10–12 minutes. Garnish with oregano sprigs and serve.

cauliflower bake

serves 4　　　　**prep: 10 mins**　　　　**cook: 40 mins**

The bright red of the tomatoes is a great contrast to the colours of the cauliflower and herbs in this dish, making it appealing to both the eye and the palate. It is easy to prepare and satisfying to eat.

INGREDIENTS

500 g/1 lb 2 oz cauliflower,
broken into florets
600 g/1 lb 5 oz potatoes, cut into cubes
100 g/3½ oz cherry tomatoes
chopped fresh flat-leaved parsley,
to garnish

SAUCE

25 g/1 oz butter or margarine
1 leek, sliced
1 garlic clove, crushed
3 tbsp plain flour
300 ml/10 fl oz milk
85 g/3 oz mixed cheese, such
as Cheddar, Parmesan and
Gruyère cheese, grated
½ tsp paprika
2 tbsp chopped fresh
flat-leaved parsley
salt and pepper

NUTRITIONAL INFORMATION

Calories 305

Protein 15g

Carbohydrate 31g

Sugars 9g

Fat 14g

Saturates 6g

variation

You can use broccoli instead of cauliflower for this dish, if you prefer. Alternatively, use a mixture of broccoli and cauliflower for a mix of colours.

cook's tip

When you choose a fresh cauliflower for this dish, look for a tightly packed flower with no brown marks or blemishes, surrounded by plenty of protective leaves.

1 Preheat the oven to 180°C/350°F/Gas Mark 4. Cook the cauliflower florets in a saucepan of boiling water for 10 minutes. Meanwhile, cook the potatoes in a separate saucepan of boiling water for 10 minutes. Drain both vegetables and reserve until required.

2 To make the sauce, melt the butter in a large saucepan. Add the leek and garlic and cook over a low heat for 1 minute. Stir in the flour and cook, stirring, for 1 minute. Remove from the heat, then gradually stir in the milk, 55 g/ 2 oz of the cheese, paprika and parsley. Return to the heat and bring to the boil, stirring. Season to taste with salt and pepper.

3 Transfer the cauliflower to a deep, ovenproof dish. Add the cherry tomatoes and top with the potatoes. Pour the sauce over to cover and sprinkle over the remaining grated cheese.

4 Cook in the preheated oven for 20 minutes, or until the vegetables are cooked through and the cheese is golden brown and bubbling. Garnish with chopped parsley and serve immediately.

potato-topped vegetables

cook: 1 hr 15 mins   **prep: 20 mins**   **serves 4**

NUTRITIONAL INFORMATION

Calories	.413
Protein	.19g
Carbohydrate	.41g
Sugars	.11g
Fat	.18g
Saturates	.11g

variation

You can parboil almost any selection of vegetables for this dish. Try stirring a handful of frozen peas into the vegetable mixture at the end of Step 2.

This is a very colourful and nutritious dish, packed full of tasty, crunchy vegetables, coated in a creamy white wine sauce.

INGREDIENTS

1 carrot, diced

175 g/6 oz cauliflower florets

175 g/6 oz broccoli florets

1 fennel bulb, sliced

85 g/3 oz French beans, halved

25 g/1 oz butter

25 g/1 oz plain flour

150 ml/5 fl oz Vegetable Stock (see page 13)

150 ml/5 fl oz dry white wine

150 ml/5 fl oz milk

175 g/6 oz chestnut mushrooms, quartered

2 tbsp chopped fresh sage

TOPPING

900 g/2 lb floury potatoes, diced

25 g/1 oz butter

4 tbsp natural yogurt

70 g/2½ oz freshly grated Parmesan cheese

1 tsp fennel seeds

salt and pepper

cook's tip

For an extra creamy topping, mash the potatoes with the butter and yogurt in Step 3, and before mashing in the cheese, beat the mixture for 1–2 minutes with a hand-held whisk.

1 Preheat the oven to 190°C/375°F/Gas Mark 5. Cook the carrot, cauliflower, broccoli, fennel and French beans in a saucepan of boiling water for 10 minutes, or until just tender. Drain and reserve.

2 Melt the butter in a separate saucepan. Stir in the flour and cook over a low heat for 1 minute. Remove from the heat and stir in the stock, wine and milk. Return to the heat and bring to the boil, stirring constantly, until thickened. Stir in the reserved vegetables, mushrooms and sage.

3 To make the topping, cook the potatoes in a large saucepan of boiling water for 10–15 minutes. Drain and mash with the butter, yogurt and half the cheese. Stir in the fennel seeds. Season to taste with salt and pepper.

4 Spoon the vegetable mixture into a 1-litre/ 1¾-pint pie dish. Spoon the potato mixture over the top, sprinkle over the remaining cheese and cook in the preheated oven for 30–35 minutes, or until golden. Serve immediately.

rice & pasta

A staple for half the world, rice is one of the most versatile of ingredients, partnering vegetables, meat, poultry, fish and shellfish with equal ease. From the United States to Thailand, almost every country in the world has its own favourite rice-based dish. Most famous of all, perhaps, are Italy's risottos, and this chapter features three very different but absolutely delicious versions, with hints and tips on how to achieve the desired creamy perfection.

Pasta and noodles also play an important role in the cuisines of the world – but most are not one-pot dishes. As a general rule, pasta and sauce are cooked separately and, although recipes may be easy, there is no getting away from using several saucepans. Well, the exception proves the rule and this chapter includes the fabulous Pasta with Garlic & Pine Kernels (see page 195), with its delicious no-cook sauce, and the scrumptious all-in-one Crisp Noodle & Vegetable Stir-fry (see page 200).

Some dishes are flavoured with meat or fish, others are vegetarian or even vegan. Delight your guests with saffron-coloured Spanish Rice with Chicken (see page 175), a mouth-watering Jambalaya (see page 184) or a luxuriously rich-tasting Risotto with Four Cheeses (see page 188). If you are in a hurry for the family supper, why not try Pork Hash (see page 180) or Pasta with Pesto (see page 202) and, if it's too hot to do much cooking, then Tricolour Pasta Salad (see page 194) is an almost instant solution.

greek chicken & rice

serves 4   **prep: 15 mins** ⏲   **cook: 40–45 mins** ♨

Look for large, slightly wrinkled Greek olives marinated in oil, and for ewe's milk feta cheese, to give this dish an authentic flavour.

INGREDIENTS

8 chicken thighs

2 tbsp sunflower oil

1 onion, chopped

2 garlic cloves, finely chopped

175 g/6 oz long-grain rice

225 ml/8 fl oz Chicken Stock
(see page 13)

800 g/1 lb 12 oz canned
chopped tomatoes

1 tbsp chopped fresh thyme

2 tbsp chopped fresh oregano

12 black olives, stoned and chopped

55 g/2 oz feta cheese, crumbled

fresh oregano sprigs, to garnish

NUTRITIONAL INFORMATION	
Calories 417	
Protein 25g	
Carbohydrate 47g	
Sugars 8g	
Fat 16g	
Saturates 3g	

cook's tip

If you can afford organic chicken, it will have a better texture and flavour than ordinary chicken. If you are using frozen chicken, check that it is thoroughly thawed before you begin cooking.

1 Remove the skin from the chicken. Heat the oil in a flameproof casserole. Add the chicken, in batches, if necessary, and cook over a medium heat, turning occasionally, for 8–10 minutes, or until golden. Transfer to a plate with a slotted spoon.

2 Add the onion, garlic, long-grain rice and about 50 ml/2 fl oz of the stock to the casserole and cook, stirring, for 5 minutes, or until the onion is softened. Pour in the remaining stock and add the tomatoes and their juices and the herbs.

3 Return the chicken thighs to the casserole, pushing them down into the rice. Bring to the boil, then reduce the heat, cover and simmer for 25–30 minutes, or until the chicken is cooked through and tender. Stir in the olives and sprinkle the cheese on top. Garnish with oregano sprigs and serve immediately.

spanish rice with chicken

cook: 1 hr 10 mins   **prep: 15 mins**   **serves 4**

Saffron gives this hearty, warming dish a lovely sunshine-yellow colour, while mild green chillies add a kick to the flavour.

NUTRITIONAL INFORMATION	
Calories	.616
Protein	.52g
Carbohydrate	.47g
Sugars	.7g
Fat	.24g
Saturates	.5g

INGREDIENTS

3 tbsp olive oil

1.25 kg/2 lb 12 oz chicken pieces

salt and pepper

2 onions, sliced

175 g/6 oz long-grain rice

125 ml/4 fl oz dry white wine

pinch of saffron threads, lightly crushed

350 ml/12 fl oz Chicken Stock
(see page 13)

1–2 mild fresh green chillies,
such as serrano

2 garlic cloves, finely chopped

2 beef tomatoes, peeled, deseeded
and chopped

fresh coriander sprigs, to garnish

variation

For extra colour, garnish the dish with 140 g/5 oz of bottled pimientos – a mild variety of pepper – cut into very thin strips.

1 Heat 2 tablespoons of the oil in a flameproof casserole. Season the chicken, add to the casserole and cook over a medium heat, turning occasionally, for 8–10 minutes, or until golden. Transfer to a plate with a slotted spoon.

2 Add the remaining oil to the casserole. Add the onions and cook over a low heat, stirring occasionally, for 5 minutes, or until translucent. Add the rice and cook, stirring, for 2 minutes, or until the grains are transparent and coated with oil.

3 Pour in the wine. Bring to the boil, then reduce the heat, cover and simmer for 8 minutes, or until all the liquid has been absorbed. Combine the saffron and stock and pour into the casserole. Stir in the chillies and garlic and season to taste with salt. Cover and simmer for 15 minutes.

4 Add the tomatoes and return the chicken pieces to the casserole, pushing them down into the rice. Cover and cook for a further 25 minutes, or until the chicken is cooked through and tender. Garnish with coriander sprigs and serve.

louisiana rice

cook: 30 mins

prep: 20 mins, plus 15 mins standing

serves 4

NUTRITIONAL INFORMATION	
Calories	.394
Protein	.26g
Carbohydrate	.36g
Sugars	.5g
Fat	.17g
Saturates	.3g

This lightly spiced, filling dish from the Deep South of America is quick, easy and economical – perfect for a midweek supper.

INGREDIENTS

4 tbsp sunflower or corn oil

225 g/8 oz fresh pork mince

1 onion, chopped

1 garlic clove, finely chopped

1 aubergine, diced

1 green pepper, deseeded and diced

2 celery sticks, chopped

1 tsp paprika

1 tsp cayenne pepper

1 tbsp chopped fresh thyme

salt and pepper

425 ml/15 fl oz Chicken Stock (see page 13)

225 g/8 oz chicken livers, minced

140 g/5 oz long-grain rice

1 bay leaf

3 tbsp chopped fresh parsley

variation

You can substitute a small courgette, chopped, for the celery, if you would prefer a milder flavour in this dish.

cook's tip

Rinsing uncooked rice in cold water helps to remove some of the starch. This ensures that the grains are less likely to stick together during cooking.

1 Heat the oil in a large, heavy-based frying pan. Add the pork and cook over a medium heat, stirring, for 8–10 minutes, or until broken up and browned all over.

2 Add the onion, garlic, aubergine, green pepper, celery, paprika, cayenne and thyme and season to taste with salt and pepper. Cover and cook, stirring frequently, for 5 minutes. Stir in the stock, scraping up any sediment on the base of the frying pan. Cover and simmer for 5 minutes.

3 Add the chicken livers and cook for 2–3 minutes. Stir in the rice and the bay leaf. Cover and simmer for 7 minutes, then remove the frying pan from the heat, but do not uncover. Leave to steam for 15 minutes, or until the rice is tender. Stir in the parsley, fluff up the rice and serve immediately.

chicken basquaise

serves 4   **prep: 15 mins**   **cook: 1 hr 20 mins**

Sweet peppers are a typical ingredient of dishes originating in the Basque region in France. In this recipe, Bayonne ham from the Pyrenees adds a delicious extra flavour.

INGREDIENTS

1 chicken, about 1.3 kg/3 lb, cut into 8 pieces

2 tbsp plain flour

salt and pepper

3 tbsp olive oil

1 Spanish onion, thickly sliced

2 red or yellow peppers, deseeded and cut lengthways into thick strips

2 garlic cloves, finely chopped

140 g/5 oz spicy chorizo sausage, peeled and cut into 1-cm/½-inch pieces

1 tbsp tomato purée

200 g/7 oz long-grain rice

450 ml/16 fl oz Chicken Stock (see page 13)

1 tsp chilli flakes

½ tsp dried thyme

115 g/4 oz Bayonne ham, diced

12 dry-cured black olives

2 tbsp chopped fresh flat-leaved parsley

TO GARNISH

lemon slices

fresh flat-leaved parsley sprigs

NUTRITIONAL INFORMATION

Calories	.559
Protein	.50g
Carbohydrate	.44g
Sugars	.8g
Fat	.21g
Saturates	.6g

variation

You can use any type of air-dried ham for this recipe, such as Ardennes or Westphalian ham, depending on what is available in your local delicatessen.

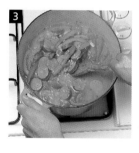

cook's tip

Browning the chicken before stewing it ensures that the meat will have an appetizing colour in the finished dish. If a recipe calls for several pieces of chicken, you can brown them in batches.

1 Pat the chicken pieces dry with kitchen paper. Place the flour in a large polythene bag, season with salt and pepper and add the chicken pieces. Seal the bag and shake to coat the chicken.

2 Heat 2 tablespoons of the oil in a flameproof casserole. Add the chicken and cook over a medium–high heat, turning frequently, for 15 minutes, or until browned. Transfer to a plate.

3 Heat the remaining oil in the casserole and add the onion and red peppers. Reduce the heat to medium and stir-fry until the onions colour and soften. Add the garlic, chorizo and tomato purée and cook, stirring, for 3 minutes, then add the rice and cook, stirring to coat, for 2 minutes, or until translucent.

4 Add the stock, chilli flakes and thyme, season to taste with salt and pepper and stir well. Bring to the boil. Return the chicken to the casserole, pressing it gently into the rice. Cover and cook over a very low heat for 45 minutes, or until the chicken is cooked through and the rice is tender.

5 Gently stir the ham, olives and half the parsley into the rice mixture. Re-cover and heat through for a further 5 minutes. Sprinkle with the remaining parsley and serve garnished with lemon slices and parsley sprigs.

pork hash

serves 4   **prep: 10 mins**   **cook: 55 mins**

This is a tasty dish for a midweek supper – once it's in the oven, you can put your feet up, relax with a glass of wine, and look forward to a filling meal with a feast of flavours.

INGREDIENTS

400 g/14 oz canned chopped tomatoes

600–700 ml/1–1¼ pints Beef Stock (see page 13)

1 tbsp sunflower oil

450 g/1 lb fresh pork mince

1 large onion, chopped

1 red pepper, deseeded and chopped

400 g/14 oz long-grain rice

1 tbsp chilli powder

450 g/1 lb fresh or frozen green beans

salt and pepper

NUTRITIONAL INFORMATION

Calories	.625
Protein	.34g
Carbohydrate	.100g
Sugars	.11g
Fat	.13g
Saturates	.3g

variation

For a beef hash, substitute beef mince for the pork, and if you prefer, use peas instead of beans.

1 Preheat the oven to 180°C/350°F/Gas Mark 4. Drain the tomatoes, reserving their juices, and reserve. Make the juices up to 850 ml/1½ pints with the stock and reserve.

2 Heat the oil in a large, flameproof casserole. Add the pork, onion and red pepper and cook over a medium heat, stirring frequently, for 8–10 minutes, or until the onion is softened and the meat is broken up and golden brown. Add the rice and cook, stirring constantly, for 2 minutes.

3 Add the tomatoes, stock mixture, chilli powder and beans to the casserole and season to taste with salt and pepper. Bring to the boil, then cover and transfer to the preheated oven to bake for 40 minutes. Serve immediately.

tuna rice

cook: 10 mins   **prep: 10 mins**   **serves 4**

This is a scrumptious way to use up leftover boiled rice. Alternatively, next time you are serving rice with a meal, cook an extra 250 g/9 oz and serve this easy dish the next day.

NUTRITIONAL INFORMATION

Calories	.460
Protein	.20g
Carbohydrate	.66g
Sugars	.1g
Fat	.14g
Saturates	.2g

INGREDIENTS

3 tbsp groundnut or sunflower oil

4 spring onions, chopped

2 garlic cloves, finely chopped

200 g/7 oz canned tuna in oil, drained and flaked

175 g/6 oz frozen or canned sweetcorn kernels and peppers

750 g/1 lb 10 oz cold boiled rice

2 tbsp Thai fish sauce

1 tbsp light soy sauce

salt and pepper

2 tbsp chopped fresh coriander, to garnish

1 Heat the groundnut oil in a preheated wok or large, heavy-based frying pan. Add the spring onions and stir-fry for 2 minutes, then add the garlic and stir-fry for a further 1 minute.

2 Add the tuna and the sweetcorn and peppers, and stir-fry for 2 minutes.

3 Add the rice, fish sauce and soy sauce and stir-fry for 2 minutes. Season to taste with salt and pepper and serve immediately, garnished with chopped coriander.

cook's tip

Leftover cooked rice should be cooled quickly, stored in the refrigerator and eaten within 24 hours. It is essential that the rice is cold and dry before you stir-fry it, otherwise it will become sticky.

azerbaijani lamb pilaf

cook: 45 mins   **prep: 15 mins**   **serves 4**

NUTRITIONAL INFORMATION	
Calories	.399
Protein	.25g
Carbohydrate	.45g
Sugars	.19g
Fat	.13g
Saturates	.4g

This type of dish is popular in the Balkans and through Russia to the Middle East. The saffron threads and pomegranate juice give it an exotic aroma, colour and flavour.

variation

This pilaf will work just as well with long-grain rice or basmati rice substituted for the arborio rice.

INGREDIENTS

2–3 tbsp vegetable oil

650 g/1 lb 7 oz boneless lamb shoulder, cut into 2.5-cm/1-inch cubes

2 onions, roughly chopped

1 tsp ground cumin

200 g/7 oz arborio rice

1 tbsp tomato purée

1 tsp saffron threads

100 ml/3½ fl oz pomegranate juice (see Cook's Tip)

850 ml/1½ pints lamb stock, Chicken Stock (see page 13) or water

115 g/4 oz no-soak dried apricots or prunes, halved

2 tbsp raisins

salt and pepper

2 tbsp chopped fresh mint

2 tbsp chopped fresh watercress

cook's tip

Pomegranate juice is available from Middle Eastern food stores. If you cannot find it, substitute unsweetened grape or apple juice.

1 Heat the oil in a large flameproof casserole or saucepan over a high heat. Add the lamb, in batches, and cook over a high heat, turning frequently, for 7 minutes, or until lightly browned.

2 Add the onions, reduce the heat to medium and cook for 2 minutes, or until beginning to soften. Add the cumin and rice and cook, stirring to coat, for 2 minutes, or until the rice is translucent. Stir in the tomato purée and the saffron threads.

3 Add the pomegranate juice and stock. Bring to the boil, stirring. Stir in the apricots and raisins. Reduce the heat to low, cover, and simmer for 20–25 minutes, or until the lamb and rice are tender and all of the liquid has been absorbed.

4 Season to taste with salt and pepper, then sprinkle the chopped mint and watercress over the pilaf and serve straight from the casserole.

jambalaya

serves 6   **prep: 20 mins**   **cook: 50–55 mins**

This Cajun dish is borrowed from Spain, where it originated. Its lively mixture of chicken and prawns makes it a good dish to serve at a brunch party, instead of the more traditional kedgeree.

INGREDIENTS

2 tbsp lard	12 Mediterranean prawns, peeled
1.5 kg/3 lb 5 oz chicken pieces	225 g/8 oz long-grain rice
25 g/1 oz plain flour	450 ml/16 fl oz Chicken Stock
225 g/8 oz rindless smoked	(see page 13) or water
gammon, diced	dash of Tabasco sauce
1 onion, chopped	salt and pepper
1 orange pepper, deseeded and sliced	3 spring onions, finely chopped
350 g/12 oz tomatoes, peeled	2 tbsp chopped fresh
and chopped	flat-leaved parsley
1 garlic clove, finely chopped	fresh flat-leaved parsley sprigs,
1 tsp chopped fresh thyme	to garnish

NUTRITIONAL INFORMATION	
Calories	.570
Protein	.59g
Carbohydrate	.42g
Sugars	.3g
Fat	.20g
Saturates	.5g

variation

If you don't want to use lard in this recipe, substitute 2 tablespoons of corn oil at the beginning of Step 1.

cook's tip

Jambalaya is a Cajun dish, the idea for which originally came from Spain. If you like an even hotter taste, add 1 teaspoon of cayenne pepper with the seasoning in Step 3.

1 Melt the lard in a large, flameproof casserole. Add the chicken and cook over a medium heat, turning occasionally, for 8–10 minutes, or until golden brown all over. Transfer the chicken to a plate with a slotted spoon.

2 Add the flour and cook over a very low heat, stirring, for 15 minutes, or until golden brown. Do not let it burn. Return the chicken pieces to the casserole with the gammon, onion, orange pepper, tomatoes, garlic and thyme. Cook, stirring frequently, for 10 minutes.

3 Stir in the prawns, rice and stock and season to taste with Tabasco, salt and pepper. Bring the mixture to the boil, reduce the heat and cook for 15–20 minutes, or until all of the liquid has been absorbed and the rice is tender. Stir in the spring onions and chopped parsley, garnish with parsley sprigs and serve immediately.

seafood risotto

cook: 30 mins   **prep: 15 mins**   **serves 4**

NUTRITIONAL INFORMATION	
Calories	.547
Protein	.46g
Carbohydrate	.60g
Sugars	.8g
Fat	.15g
Saturates	.6g

The secret of a successful risotto is to use round grain Italian rice, such as arborio, and to add a ladleful of stock at a time, making sure that it is fully absorbed before more is added.

INGREDIENTS

350 g/12 oz skinless cod fillet

25 g/1 oz unsalted butter

1 onion, chopped

2 red peppers, deseeded and chopped

4 tomatoes, peeled, deseeded and chopped

8 ready-prepared scallops

2 tbsp olive oil

225 g/8 oz risotto rice

450 ml/16 fl oz hot Fish Stock (see page 13)

salt

225 g/8 oz cooked peeled prawns

1 tbsp chopped flat-leaved parsley

2 tbsp freshly grated Parmesan cheese

fresh parsley sprigs, to garnish

variation

You can substitute chunks of monkfish for the cod to give the dish a slightly meatier texture, if you prefer.

cook's tip

Risotto rice will absorb stock more readily if the stock is kept at simmering point in another saucepan while it is being added in Step 2.

1 Cut the fish into cubes. Melt half the butter in a large saucepan. Add the onion, red peppers and tomatoes and cook over a low heat, stirring occasionally, for 5 minutes, or until softened. Add the fish and scallops, and cook for a further 3 minutes. Transfer the fish mixture to a plate with a slotted spoon, cover and reserve.

2 Add the oil to the pan and heat gently. Add the rice and stir to coat with the butter and oil. Stir in a ladleful of stock and season to taste with salt. Cook, stirring, until the stock has been absorbed. Continue cooking and adding stock, a ladleful at a time, for 20 minutes, or until the rice is tender and all of the liquid has been absorbed.

3 Gently stir in the reserved fish mixture with the prawns and heat through for 2 minutes. Transfer the risotto to a warmed serving dish, sprinkle with the chopped parsley and Parmesan cheese and serve immediately, garnished with parsley sprigs.

risotto with four cheeses

serves 4　　　　**prep: 15 mins** ⏲　　　　**cook: 30 mins** ⏲

Rich and with a subtle flavour, this is a classic Italian dish that would normally be served before the main course.

INGREDIENTS

55 g/2 oz Taleggio cheese

55 g/2 oz Fontina cheese

55 g/2 oz Parmesan cheese

55 g/2 oz Gorgonzola cheese

40 g/1½ oz unsalted butter

1 onion, finely chopped

350 g/12 oz risotto rice

200 ml/7 fl oz dry white wine

1 litre/1¾ pints hot Vegetable Stock (see page 13)

salt and pepper

fresh flat-leaved parsley sprigs, to garnish

NUTRITIONAL INFORMATION	
Calories	.425
Protein	.14g
Carbohydrate	.53g
Sugars	.2g
Fat	.17g
Saturates	.11g

variation

You can use other cheeses for this risotto, but try to get a mixture of flavours. Try a combination of dolcelatte, Gruyère, buffalo mozzarella and pecorino.

1 Grate the Taleggio, Fontina and Parmesan cheeses and crumble the Gorgonzola cheese, then reserve until required.

2 Melt the butter in a large saucepan, add the onion and cook over a low heat, stirring occasionally, for 5 minutes, or until softened. Add the rice and stir to coat the grains with butter. Add the wine and cook until almost all of it has been absorbed.

3 Add a ladleful of stock and cook, stirring, until the liquid has been absorbed. Continue cooking and adding the stock, a ladleful at a time, for 20 minutes, or until the rice is tender and all of the liquid has been absorbed.

4 Turn off the heat and stir in the Gorgonzola, Taleggio, Fontina and one-quarter of the Parmesan cheese, until melted. Season to taste with salt and pepper. Transfer the risotto to a serving dish, sprinkle with the remaining Parmesan cheese, garnish with parsley sprigs and serve immediately.

risotto primavera

cook: 30 mins   **prep: 10 mins**   **serves 4**

As evenings get longer, the days grow warmer and the first spring vegetables ripen, this is the ideal choice for a midweek supper.

NUTRITIONAL INFORMATION

Calories	399
Protein	11g
Carbohydrate	54g
Sugars	4g
Fat	16g
Saturates	7g

INGREDIENTS

115 g/4 oz asparagus spears, cut into short lengths

2 young carrots, thinly sliced

25 g/1 oz unsalted butter

2 tbsp olive oil

1 white onion, chopped

2 garlic cloves, finely chopped

225 g/8 oz risotto rice

3 tbsp dry white wine

1 litre/1¾ pints hot Vegetable Stock (see page 13)

55 g/2 oz button mushrooms, halved

salt and pepper

55 g/2 oz freshly grated Parmesan cheese, to serve

cook's tip

White onions, which are very popular in Italy, are sweeter and milder than brown onions. Alternatively, you could use a red onion for this dish.

1 Blanch the asparagus and carrots in a large saucepan of boiling water and drain well.

2 Melt the butter with the oil in a large, heavy-based saucepan. Add the onion and garlic and cook over a low heat, stirring occasionally, for 5 minutes, or until softened. Add the rice and stir well to coat the grains with the butter and oil mixture. Add the white wine and cook until the liquid has been fully absorbed.

3 Add a ladleful of stock to the rice and cook, stirring, until the liquid has been absorbed. Continue cooking and adding the stock, a ladleful at a time, for 20 minutes, or until the rice is tender and all of the liquid has been absorbed.

4 Gently stir in the asparagus, carrots and mushrooms, season to taste with salt and pepper and cook for a further 2 minutes, or until heated through. Serve immediately, handing the Parmesan cheese separately.

rice & peas

serves 4   **prep: 15 mins**   **cook: 30 mins**

This is a famous dish from the Veneto region of Italy, known as Risi e Bisi. Pancetta is cured belly of pork – this is the Italian equivalent of unsmoked bacon, and it is available from some large supermarkets and from Italian delicatessens.

INGREDIENTS

55 g/2 oz unsalted butter	250 g/9 oz fresh peas
1 tbsp olive oil	salt and pepper
1 red onion, chopped	200 g/7 oz risotto rice
1 garlic clove, finely chopped	3 tbsp chopped fresh
55 g/2 oz pancetta, chopped	flat-leaved parsley
1.4 litres/2½ pints Chicken Stock	55 g/2 oz Parmesan cheese
(see page 13)	Parmesan cheese shavings, to garnish

NUTRITIONAL INFORMATION	
Calories	.484
Protein	.15g
Carbohydrate	.52g
Sugars	.4g
Fat	.25g
Saturates	.13g

variation

To use frozen peas, add them with the parsley in Step 3, but before adding the butter and cheese, cook for 5 minutes, until tender.

cook's tip

Try to use fresh rather than frozen peas for this recipe if at all possible. Much of the charm of the dish comes from their tenderness and freshness.

1 Melt half the butter with the olive oil in a large, heavy-based saucepan. Add the onion, garlic and pancetta and cook over a low heat, stirring occasionally, for 5 minutes, or until the onion has softened.

2 Add the stock and peas and season to taste with salt and pepper. Bring the mixture to the boil. Add the rice, return to the boil, then reduce the heat and simmer, stirring occasionally, for 20 minutes, or until the rice is tender.

3 Meanwhile, grate the Parmesan cheese and reserve until required. Add the parsley to the saucepan and stir in the remaining butter and the freshly grated Parmesan cheese. When the cheese has melted, transfer to a warmed dish, garnish with the Parmesan cheese shavings and serve immediately.

lentil & rice casserole

serves 4   **prep: 15 mins**   **cook: 40 mins**

This is a really hearty dish, perfect for winter days when a substantial hot dish is just what you need to keep the cold out.

INGREDIENTS

225 g/8 oz red split lentils, rinsed

55 g/2 oz long-grain rice

1.2 litres/2 pints Vegetable Stock (see page 13)

1 leek, cut into chunks

3 garlic cloves, crushed

400 g/14 oz canned chopped tomatoes

1 tsp each of ground cumin, chilli powder and garam masala

1 red pepper, deseeded and sliced

100 g/3½ oz small broccoli florets

8 baby corn cobs, halved lengthways

55 g/2 oz French beans, halved

1 tbsp shredded fresh basil

salt and pepper

fresh basil sprigs, to garnish

NUTRITIONAL INFORMATION

Calories	.312
Protein	.20g
Carbohydrate	.51g
Sugars	.9g
Fat	.2g
Saturates	.0.4g

variation

You can vary the rice in this recipe – instead of the long-grain rice, use brown or wild rice, if you prefer.

1 Place the lentils, rice and Vegetable Stock in a flameproof casserole and cook over a low heat, stirring occasionally, for 20 minutes.

2 Add the leek and garlic to the saucepan with the tomatoes and their juices, ground spices, red pepper, broccoli, baby corn and French beans and stir well to mix.

3 Bring the mixture to the boil, then reduce the heat, cover and simmer for a further 10–15 minutes, or until the vegetables are tender.

4 Add the shredded basil and season to taste with salt and pepper. Garnish with basil sprigs and serve.

linguine with tomato sauce

cook: 10 mins

**prep: 10 mins,
plus 30 mins marinating**

serves 4

*The best time to cook this dish is in the middle of summer – you
should use large, sun-ripened tomatoes for the fabulous fresh sauce.*

NUTRITIONAL INFORMATION	
Calories	.683
Protein	.15g
Carbohydrate	.88g
Sugars	.8g
Fat	.33g
Saturates	.4g

INGREDIENTS

4 large tomatoes, peeled,
deseeded and diced
2 garlic cloves, finely chopped
8 fresh basil leaves, shredded
1 tbsp chopped fresh parsley
1 tbsp chopped fresh oregano
150 ml/5 fl oz extra virgin olive oil
salt and pepper
450 g/1 lb dried linguine
115 g/4 oz stoned black olives, chopped

TO SERVE

baby lamb's lettuce
shredded beetroot

variation

You can serve any long
pasta, such as spaghetti,
with this sauce. If you use
fresh pasta, cook for only
2–3 minutes after the
water returns to the boil.

1 Place the tomatoes in a shallow, non-metallic dish. Add the garlic, basil, parsley, oregano and oil and season to taste with salt and pepper. Mix well, cover with clingfilm and leave to marinate for 30 minutes.

2 Bring a large saucepan of lightly salted water to the boil. Add the pasta, return to the boil and cook for 8–10 minutes, or until tender but still firm to the bite. Drain the pasta and return it to the saucepan.

3 Add the tomatoes with their marinade and the olives. Toss well and serve with baby lamb's lettuce and shredded beetroot.

tricolour pasta salad

serves 4 **prep: 10 mins** **cook: 10 mins**

This prettily coloured salad is full of lovely, refreshing flavours – tomatoes, cheese, avocado, basil and pine kernels.

INGREDIENTS

salt and pepper

175 g/6 oz dried fusilli

1 avocado

6 tomatoes, thinly sliced

225 g/8 oz mozzarella cheese, thinly sliced

2 tbsp toasted pine kernels

fresh basil leaves, to garnish

DRESSING

6 tbsp extra virgin olive oil

2 tbsp white wine vinegar

1 tsp Dijon mustard

2 tbsp shredded fresh basil leaves

pinch of sugar

NUTRITIONAL INFORMATION	
Calories	593
Protein	22g
Carbohydrate	39g
Sugars	7g
Fat	40g
Saturates	12g

cook's tip

Do not peel the avocado in advance of preparing and serving the salad, because the flesh quickly discolours on exposure to the air.

1 Bring a large saucepan of lightly salted water to the boil. Add the pasta, return to the boil and cook for 8–10 minutes, or until tender but still firm to the bite. Drain, refresh under cold running water and drain again.

2 To make the dressing, whisk the oil, vinegar, mustard, basil and sugar together in a small bowl until combined. Season to taste with salt and pepper.

3 Cut the avocado in half and remove the stone. Peel, then thinly slice the flesh lengthways.

4 Arrange the slices of avocado, tomato and mozzarella cheese, overlapping slightly, around the outside of a large serving platter. Add half the dressing to the pasta, toss well, then spoon into the centre of the platter. Pour the remaining dressing over the salad, sprinkle with the pine kernels, garnish with basil leaves and serve.

pasta with garlic & pine kernels

cook: 10 mins **prep: 10 mins** **serves 4**

*When you are in a hurry, pasta is the answer. This tasty sauce can
be prepared while the pasta is cooking to make a meal in minutes.*

NUTRITIONAL INFORMATION	
Calories	.397
Protein	.10g
Carbohydrate	.48g
Sugars	.3g
Fat	.20g
Saturates	.2g

INGREDIENTS

salt and pepper

250 g/9 oz dried elicoidali or penne

3 garlic cloves, roughly chopped

2 canned anchovy fillets, drained
and roughly chopped

2 tbsp bottled capers, drained
and finely chopped

1 tsp tarragon mustard

50 ml/2 fl oz extra virgin olive oil

4 tbsp chopped mixed fresh herbs,
such as tarragon, chives and
flat-leaved parsley

55 g/2 oz toasted pine kernels

1 tbsp lemon juice

Parmesan cheese shavings, to garnish

cook's tip

Time the pasta from the
moment when the water
returns to the boil and begin
testing when it has been
boiling for 8 minutes. Test by
breaking off a small piece and
biting it with your front teeth.

1 Bring a large saucepan
of lightly salted water
to the boil. Add the pasta,
return to the boil and cook for
8–10 minutes, or until tender
but still firm to the bite.

2 Meanwhile, put the
garlic and anchovies
into a mortar and pound with
a pestle to make a paste.
Scrape the paste into a bowl

and stir in the capers and
tarragon mustard.

3 Gradually stir in the oil,
then add the chopped
fresh herbs, toasted pine
kernels and lemon juice and
season the mixture to taste
with salt and pepper.

4 Drain the pasta
thoroughly and return
it to the saucepan. Add the
sauce and toss well to coat
the pasta. Serve immediately,
garnished with Parmesan
cheese shavings.

cashew nut paella

serves 4 **prep: 15 mins** **cook: 35 mins**

Paella traditionally contains chicken and fish, but this recipe is packed with vegetables and nuts for a truly delicious and simple vegetarian dish.

INGREDIENTS

2 tbsp olive oil

1 tbsp butter

1 red onion, chopped

150 g/5½ oz arborio rice

1 tsp ground turmeric

1 tsp ground cumin

½ tsp chilli powder

3 garlic cloves, crushed

1 fresh green chilli, sliced

1 green pepper, deseeded and diced

1 red pepper, deseeded and diced

75 g/2¾ oz baby corn cobs, halved lengthways

2 tbsp stoned black olives

1 large tomato, deseeded and diced

450 ml/16 fl oz Vegetable Stock (see page 13)

75 g/2¾ oz unsalted cashew nuts

50 g/1¾ oz frozen peas

2 tbsp chopped fresh parsley

pinch of cayenne pepper

salt and pepper

fresh flat-leaved parsley sprigs, to garnish

NUTRITIONAL INFORMATION	
Calories	.406
Protein	.10g
Carbohydrate	.44g
Sugars	.8g
Fat	.22g
Saturates	.6g

variation

Replace the cashew nuts with the same amount of roasted peanuts and use a red chilli instead of green, if you prefer.

cook's tip

Always buy firm, shiny and heavy fresh chillies. Remove the packaging and store in the refrigerator, otherwise they tend to become limp very quickly.

1 Heat the olive oil and butter in a large frying pan or paella pan until the butter has melted.

2 Add the onion to the frying pan and cook over a medium heat, stirring constantly, for 2–3 minutes, or until the onion has softened.

3 Stir in the rice, turmeric, ground cumin, chilli powder, garlic, sliced chilli, peppers, baby corn, black olives and diced tomato and cook over a medium heat, stirring occasionally, for 1–2 minutes.

4 Pour in the Vegetable Stock and bring the mixture to the boil. Reduce the heat and cook, stirring constantly, for 20 minutes.

5 Add the cashew nuts and peas and cook, stirring occasionally, for 5 minutes. Season to taste with salt and pepper and sprinkle with chopped parsley and cayenne pepper. Transfer to serving plates, garnish with parsley sprigs and serve.

vegetable lasagne

⏱ **cook: 55 mins**

⏲ **prep: 15 mins, plus 20 mins standing**

serves 4

NUTRITIONAL INFORMATION	
Calories	544
Protein	20g
Carbohydrate	61g
Sugars	18g
Fat	26g
Saturates	12g

variation

Substitute blanched, bite-sized lengths of asparagus spears for the celery sticks, for a slightly different flavour.

This colourful and tasty lasagne has layers of vegetables in tomato sauce and aubergines, all topped with a rich cheese sauce.

INGREDIENTS

1 large aubergine, sliced	2 tbsp chopped fresh basil
salt and pepper	8 no-pre-cook lasagne verdi sheets
3 tbsp olive oil	
2 garlic cloves, crushed	CHEESE SAUCE
1 red onion, halved and sliced	2 tbsp butter or margarine
3 mixed peppers, deseeded and diced	1 tbsp flour
225 g/8 oz mixed mushrooms, sliced	150 ml/5 fl oz Vegetable Stock
2 celery sticks, sliced	(see page 13)
1 courgette, diced	300 ml/10 fl oz milk
½ tsp chilli powder	75 g/2¾ oz Cheddar cheese, grated
½ tsp ground cumin	1 tsp Dijon mustard
2 tomatoes, chopped	1 tbsp chopped fresh basil
300 ml/10 fl oz passata	1 egg, beaten

cook's tip

Dijon mustard is one of the best types to use for a cheese sauce. It is a very hot mustard, and its heat brings out the flavour of the cheese.

1 Preheat the oven to 180°C/350°F/Gas Mark 4. Place the aubergine slices in a colander, sprinkle with salt and leave to stand for 20 minutes. Rinse under cold running water, drain and reserve until required.

2 Heat the oil in a large frying pan. Add the garlic and onion and cook over a medium heat for 1–2 minutes. Add the peppers, mushrooms, celery and courgette and cook, stirring constantly, for a further 3–4 minutes.

3 Stir in the spices and cook for 1 minute. Stir in the chopped tomatoes, passata and basil and season the mixture to taste with salt and pepper.

4 To make the sauce, melt the butter in a saucepan, stir in the flour and cook for 1 minute. Remove from the heat, stir in the stock and milk, then return to the heat and stir in half the cheese and the mustard. Bring the sauce to the boil, stirring, until thickened. Stir in the basil, then remove from the heat and stir in the egg.

5 Place half the lasagne sheets in an ovenproof dish. Top with half the vegetable mixture, then half the aubergines. Repeat the layers and spoon the cheese sauce over the top. Sprinkle the lasagne with the remaining cheese and cook in the preheated oven for 40 minutes, or until the topping is golden. Serve immediately.

crisp noodle & vegetable stir-fry

serves 4   **prep: 5 mins** ⟲   **cook: 15–20 mins** ⏱

*Once you have chopped the vegetables, this dish is quick and easy
to put together, and makes an attractive and nutritious meal for the
family, or for visitors expecting a bite to eat.*

INGREDIENTS

groundnut or sunflower oil,
for deep-frying

115 g/4 oz rice vermicelli,
broken into 7.5-cm/3-inch lengths

115 g/4 oz green beans,
cut into short lengths

2 carrots, cut into thin batons

2 courgettes, cut into thin batons

115 g/4 oz shiitake mushrooms, sliced

2.5-cm/1-inch piece fresh root
ginger, shredded

½ small head Chinese leaves, shredded

4 spring onions, shredded

85 g/3 oz beansprouts

2 tbsp dark soy sauce

2 tbsp Chinese rice wine

large pinch of sugar

2 tbsp roughly chopped fresh coriander

NUTRITIONAL INFORMATION	
Calories	.240
Protein	.7g
Carbohydrate	.33g
Sugars	.6g
Fat	.9g
Saturates	.1g

variation

For a spicier version of this dish, add
1 deseeded and sliced fresh red chilli
with the shredded ginger in Step 2.

cook's tip

This dish also looks attractive
if you serve the noodles in
a small nest on top of the
stir-fried vegetables, rather
than tossing them with the
vegetables in Step 3.

1 Half-fill a preheated
wok or deep, heavy-
based frying pan with oil. Heat
to 180–190°C/350–375°F, or
until a cube of bread browns
in 30 seconds. Add the
noodles, in batches, and cook
for 1½–2 minutes, or until crisp
and puffed up. Remove and
drain on kitchen paper. Pour
off all but 2 tablespoons of oil
from the wok.

2 Heat the remaining oil
over a high heat, then
add the green beans and stir-
fry for 2 minutes. Add the
carrot and courgette batons,
sliced mushrooms and ginger
and stir-fry for a further
2 minutes. Add the shredded
Chinese leaves and spring
onions with the beansprouts
and stir-fry for a further
1 minute.

3 Add the soy sauce,
Chinese rice wine
and sugar and cook, stirring
constantly, for 1 minute.
Add the noodles and chopped
coriander and toss well.
Serve immediately.

pasta with pesto

serves 4 **prep: 10–15 mins** **cook: 10 mins**

Traditionally, the Genoese make this delicious sauce with a pestle and mortar. The taste of this fresh pesto will be a revelation.

INGREDIENTS

salt

450 g/1 lb dried tagliatelle

fresh basil sprigs, to garnish

PESTO

2 garlic cloves

25 g/1 oz pine kernels

sea salt

115 g/4 oz fresh basil leaves

125 ml/4 fl oz olive oil

55 g/2 oz freshly grated
Parmesan cheese

NUTRITIONAL INFORMATION	
Calories	.705
Protein	.21g
Carbohydrate	.85g
Sugars	.4g
Fat	.34g
Saturates	.6g

cook's tip

To store pesto, place it in a screw-top jar, cover the surface with a layer of olive oil and keep in the refrigerator for up to 1 month.

1 To make the pesto, place the garlic, pine kernels and a large pinch of sea salt in a blender or food processor and process briefly. Add the basil leaves and process to a paste.

2 With the motor running, gradually add the oil. Scrape into a bowl and beat in the cheese. Season to taste with salt. Alternatively, put the garlic, pine kernels, a large pinch of sea salt and basil leaves into a mortar and crush with a pestle to make a paste. Transfer to a bowl, work in the Parmesan cheese, then gradually add the oil, beating with a wooden spoon. Season to taste with salt.

3 Bring a large saucepan of lightly salted water to the boil. Add the pasta, return to the boil and cook for 8–10 minutes, or until tender but still firm to the bite. Drain well, return to the saucepan and toss with half the pesto, then divide between warmed serving plates and top with the remaining pesto. Garnish with basil sprigs and serve.

macaroni cheese & tomato

⏱ **cook: 35–50 mins**   ⏲ **prep: 15 mins**   **serves 4**

This is a really simple, family dish which is inexpensive and easy to prepare and cook. Serve with a salad or fresh green vegetables.

NUTRITIONAL INFORMATION	
Calories	.592
Protein	.28g
Carbohydrate	.57g
Sugars	.6g
Fat	.29g
Saturates	.17g

INGREDIENTS

225 g/8 oz dried elbow macaroni

175 g/6 oz grated Cheddar cheese

100 g/3½ oz grated Parmesan cheese

4 tbsp fresh white breadcrumbs

1 tbsp chopped fresh basil

1 tbsp butter, plus extra for greasing

TOMATO SAUCE

1 tbsp olive oil

1 shallot, finely chopped

2 garlic cloves, crushed

500 g/1 lb 2 oz canned tomatoes

1 tbsp chopped fresh basil

salt and pepper

variation

Substitute the macaroni with dried penne or fusilli and use wholemeal breadcrumbs instead of white, if you prefer.

1 Preheat the oven to 190°C/375°F/Gas Mark 5. To make the tomato sauce, heat the oil in a heavy-based saucepan. Add the shallots and garlic and cook for 1 minute. Add the tomatoes and basil and season to taste with salt and pepper. Cook over a medium heat, stirring constantly, for 10 minutes.

2 Meanwhile, bring a large saucepan of lightly salted water to the boil. Add the macaroni and cook for 8 minutes, or until tender but still firm to the bite. Drain thoroughly and reserve.

3 Mix the cheeses together in a bowl. Grease a deep, ovenproof dish. Spoon one-third of the tomato sauce into the base of the dish, top with one-third of the macaroni and then one-third of the cheeses. Season to taste with salt and pepper. Repeat these layers twice, ending with a layer of cheese.

4 Mix the breadcrumbs and basil together and sprinkle evenly over the top. Dot the topping with butter and cook in the preheated oven for 25 minutes, or until the topping is golden brown and bubbling. Serve immediately.

italian fish stew

cook: 25 mins **prep: 5–10 mins** **serves 4**

NUTRITIONAL INFORMATION

Calories 236

Protein 20g

Carbohydrate 25g

Sugars 4g

Fat 7g

Saturates 1g

This robust stew is full of Mediterranean flavours. The firm white fish will keep its shape when cooked, making the dish look filling and appetizing – perfect for a warming meal on a chilly evening.

INGREDIENTS

2 tbsp olive oil

2 red onions, finely chopped

1 garlic clove, crushed

2 courgettes, sliced

400 g/14 oz canned chopped tomatoes

850 ml/1½ pints Fish or Vegetable Stock (see page 13)

85 g/3 oz dried pasta shapes

1 tbsp chopped fresh basil

1 tsp grated lemon rind

350 g/12 oz firm, skinless white fish fillets, such as cod, haddock or hake, cut into chunks

1 tbsp cornflour

1 tbsp water

salt and pepper

fresh basil sprigs, to garnish

variation

Substitute 1 tablespoon chopped fresh oregano or 1 teaspoon dried oregano for the chopped basil, if you prefer, and garnish the dish with fresh oregano.

cook's tip

Make sure that the fish fillets are free of bones by running your fingers over them to feel for anything sharp and removing any bones with a pair of tweezers.

1 Heat the oil in a large saucepan. Add the onions and garlic and cook over a low heat, stirring occasionally, for 5 minutes, or until softened. Add the courgettes and cook, stirring frequently, for 2–3 minutes.

2 Add the tomatoes and stock to the saucepan and bring to the boil. Add the pasta. Return to the boil, then reduce the heat, cover and simmer for 5 minutes.

3 Add the basil, lemon rind and fish chunks to the saucepan and simmer for 5 minutes, or until the fish is cooked and flakes easily when tested with the point of a knife, and the pasta is tender but still firm to the bite.

4 Blend the cornflour with the water to make a smooth paste and stir into the stew. Cook gently for 2 minutes, stirring constantly, until thickened. Season to taste with salt and pepper.

5 Ladle the stew into 4 warmed soup bowls. Garnish with basil sprigs and serve immediately.

seafood lasagne

serves 4 **prep: 30 mins,** ⏲ **plus 10 mins standing** **cook: 1 hr 10 mins** ⏲

A rich dish of layers of pasta, with seafood and mushrooms in a tomato sauce, topped with béchamel sauce and baked until golden.

INGREDIENTS

3½ tbsp butter, plus extra for greasing

5 tbsp flour

1 tsp mustard powder

600 ml/1 pint milk

2 tbsp olive oil

1 onion, chopped

2 garlic cloves, finely chopped

450 g/1 lb mixed mushrooms, sliced

150 ml/5 fl oz white wine

400 g/14 oz canned chopped tomatoes

salt and pepper

450 g/1 lb skinless white fish fillets

225 g/8 oz ready-prepared fresh scallops

4–6 sheets fresh lasagne

225 g/8 oz mozzarella cheese, chopped

NUTRITIONAL INFORMATION	
Calories	.696
Protein	.58g
Carbohydrate	.38g
Sugars	.14g
Fat	.33g
Saturates	.3g

cook's tip

For the best consistency and flavour, it is best to buy fresh pasta from an Italian delicatessen where it is made on the premises, rather than from a large supermarket.

1 Preheat the oven to 200°C/400°F/Gas Mark 6. Melt the butter in a saucepan over a low heat. Add the flour and mustard powder and stir until smooth. Simmer gently for 2 minutes without colouring. Gradually add the milk, whisking until smooth. Bring to the boil, reduce the heat and simmer for 2 minutes. Remove from the heat and reserve. Cover the surface of the sauce with clingfilm to prevent a skin forming.

2 Heat the oil in a frying pan. Add the onion and garlic and cook gently for 5 minutes, or until softened. Add the mushrooms and cook for 5 minutes, or until softened. Stir in the wine and boil rapidly until almost evaporated, then stir in the tomatoes. Bring to the boil, reduce the heat and simmer, covered, for 15 minutes. Season and reserve.

3 Cut the fish into cubes. Grease a lasagne dish, spoon half the tomato mixture over the base, top with half the fish and scallops and layer half the lasagne over the top. Pour over half the white sauce and sprinkle over half the mozzarella. Repeat these layers, finishing with sauce and mozzarella.

4 Bake in the preheated oven for 35–40 minutes, or until golden and the fish is cooked through. Remove from the oven and leave to stand for 10 minutes before serving.

seafood spaghetti

⏲ **cook: 30 mins**   ⏱ **prep: 20 mins**   **serves 4**

You can use whatever combination of shellfish you like in this recipe – it is served with freshly cooked spaghetti.

NUTRITIONAL INFORMATION	
Calories	.372
Protein	.33g
Carbohydrate	.45g
Sugars	.3g
Fat	.5g
Saturates	.1g

INGREDIENTS

450 g/1 lb fresh mussels

225 g/8 oz baby squid

225 g/8 oz fresh prawns

8 small cooked crab claws

2 tsp olive oil

1 small red onion, finely chopped

1 tbsp lemon juice

1 garlic clove, crushed

2 celery sticks, finely chopped

150 ml/5 fl oz Fish Stock (see page 13)

150 ml/5 fl oz dry white wine

small bunch of fresh tarragon

225 g/8 oz dried spaghetti

salt and pepper

2 tbsp chopped fresh tarragon, to garnish

cook's tip

Crab claws contain lean crabmeat. If you can, ask your fishmonger to crack the claws for you, leaving the pincers intact, because the shell is very tough.

1 Prepare the mussels (see page 122) and the squid (see page 132), peel and devein the prawns and crack and peel the cooked crab claws. Reserve the seafood.

2 Heat the oil in a large saucepan. Add the onion, lemon juice, garlic and celery and cook for 3–4 minutes, or until softened.

3 Pour in the stock and wine. Bring to the boil and add the tarragon and mussels. Cover and simmer for 5 minutes. Add the prawns, squid and crab claws, stir and cook for 3–4 minutes, or until the mussels have opened, the prawns are pink and the squid is opaque. Remove and discard the tarragon and any mussels that have not opened.

4 Meanwhile, bring a large saucepan of water to the boil. Add the pasta, return to the boil and cook for 10 minutes, or until tender but still firm to the bite. Drain well, add it to the shellfish mixture and toss together, then season to taste with salt and pepper.

5 Transfer the spaghetti to warmed serving plates and spoon over the cooking juices. Garnish with chopped tarragon and serve.

desserts

For many cooks, dessert is one course too far, but for many diners, it is a fine finale to a meal. Compromise with this delightful selection of one-pot sweet dishes. Why bother with a conventional – and boring – fruit pie when, with far less effort and washing-up, you could make Clafoutis (see page 243), a melt-in-the-mouth combination of succulent cherries and crispy batter, or Tarte Tatin (see page 216), an all-in-one upside-down apple pie?

Whatever the season and whatever the occasion, you will find the perfect dish to round off your meal – whether an alfresco lunch, a midwinter supper or a sophisticated dinner party. There are lots of child-friendly treats for family suppers, from Pancake Pieces (see page 245) to Apple Fritters (see page 249), as well as some delicious dishes for the more adult palate, from Syllabub (see page 232) to liqueur-laced Saucy Ice Creams (see page 253). Fruit features in many forms – hot Flambéed Peaches (see page 233) contrast with ice-cold Forest Fruits Granita (see page 251), with Warm Fruit Compote (see page 242) somewhere in between.

There are also recipes for traditional, familiar and well-loved desserts, such as Creamed Rice Pudding (see page 219) and Zabaglione (see page 230). There are light-as-air confections and substantial puddings, to make sure that even the heartiest appetite is finally satisfied.

minted pears

serves 4 **prep: 10 mins, plus** ⟳ **cook: 35–40 mins** ⟳
1–2 hrs cooling/chilling

These sweet pears are straightforward to make and taste delicious.
They can be made in advance and left to chill, making them an
ideal, easy dessert after a more complex main meal.

INGREDIENTS

4 large pears

4 tbsp caster sugar

4 tbsp clear honey

2 tbsp green crème de menthe

fresh mint sprigs, to decorate

NUTRITIONAL INFORMATION	
Calories 250	
Protein 1g	
Carbohydrate 62g	
Sugars 62g	
Fat 0g	
Saturates 0g	

cook's tip

Choose firm, ripe pears that
will hold their shape when
poached, and leave the stalks
intact when peeling for an
attractive finished dish.

1 Peel the pears and
stand them upright in
a heavy-based saucepan. Add
enough water to cover. Bring
to the boil, then reduce the
heat, cover and simmer for
25–30 minutes, or until the
pears are tender. Pour away
half the cooking water, then
add the caster sugar to the
saucepan and simmer for a
further 10 minutes.

2 Transfer the pears to
a bowl with a slotted
spoon. Pour 150 ml/5 fl oz
of the cooking water into a
measuring jug and stir in the
honey and crème de menthe.
Pour the syrup over the pears.

3 Set the pears aside to
cool, then cover with
clingfilm and chill in the
refrigerator for 1–2 hours.

Transfer the pears to individual
serving bowls, spoon the mint
syrup over them and serve
decorated with fresh mint.

spun sugar pears

cook: 40 mins   **prep: 20 mins, plus 20 mins cooling**   **serves 4**

Whole pears poached in a Madeira syrup, then served inside a delicate case of spun sugar, make a stunningly attractive dessert, which is bound to cause a stir at any dinner party.

NUTRITIONAL INFORMATION	
Calories	.166
Protein	.0.3g
Carbohydrate	.41g
Sugars	.41g
Fat	.0g
Saturates	.0g

INGREDIENTS

150 ml/5 fl oz water

150 ml/5 fl oz sweet Madeira wine

115 g/4 oz caster sugar

2 tbsp lime juice

4 ripe pears

fresh mint sprigs, to decorate

SPUN SUGAR

115 g/4 oz caster sugar

3 tbsp water

cook's tip

The caramelized sugar stiffens slightly when it is left to stand after cooking. This should make it easier to handle when you spin it around the pear. Work quickly, from the bottom of the pear upwards.

1 Mix the water, Madeira, sugar and lime juice in a deep flameproof dish or large saucepan. Cook over a high heat for 3 minutes, stirring constantly, until the sugar dissolves.

2 Peel the pears and cut a thin slice from the base of each, so that they stand upright. Place them in the dish and spoon the wine syrup over them. Cover, bring to the boil, then reduce the heat and simmer for 10 minutes, or until the pears are tender, turning them over occasionally. Leave the pears and syrup, covered, to cool.

3 Remove the cooled pears from the syrup and place on serving plates.

Bring the syrup to the boil, uncovered, then reduce the heat and simmer for 15 minutes, or until reduced by half and thickened slightly. Leave to stand for 5 minutes, then spoon over the pears.

4 To make the spun sugar, place the sugar and water in a saucepan and cook over a high heat for 6–7 minutes, stirring constantly, until the sugar has dissolved and caramelized. Leave to stand for 2 minutes.

5 Dip a teaspoon in the caramel and spin around each pear in a circular motion. Decorate with mint and serve.

exotic fruit parcels

cook: 15–20 mins

**prep: 10 mins,
plus 30 mins marinating**

serves 4

NUTRITIONAL INFORMATION	
Calories	.43
Protein	.2g
Carbohydrate	.9g
Sugars	.9g
Fat	.0.3g
Saturates	.0.1g

variation

Grenadine is a sweet syrup made from pomegranates. If you prefer you could use pomegranate juice instead (see Cook's Tip).

Delicious pieces of fresh exotic fruit are warmed through in a scented sauce to make this fabulous barbecued dessert. Silver foil parcels and sliced star fruit add a touch of glamour.

INGREDIENTS

1 papaya	3 tbsp orange juice
1 mango	single cream or low-fat
1 star fruit	natural yogurt, to serve
1 tbsp grenadine	

cook's tip

To extract the juice from a pomegranate for the variation on this recipe, cut the fruit in half and squeeze gently with a lemon squeezer – do not press too hard or the juice may become bitter.

1 Preheat the barbecue. Cut the papaya in half, scoop out the seeds and discard them. Peel the papaya and cut the flesh into thick slices.

2 Slice the mango in half lengthways around the flat stone, then cut the flesh carefully away from the stone. Score each mango half in a criss-cross pattern. Push each half inside-out to separate the cubes, then cut them away from the peel.

3 Thickly slice the star fruit. Place it in a bowl with the papaya and mango and mix. Stir the grenadine and orange juice together, pour over the fruit and leave to marinate for 30 minutes.

4 Divide the marinaded fruit between 4 double-thickness squares of foil. Gather up the edges to enclose the fruit in parcels.

5 Place the foil parcels on a grill rack set over warm coals and barbecue the fruit for 15–20 minutes. Serve in the parcel, handing the cream or yogurt separately.

banana empanadas

serves 4   **prep: 10 mins**   **cook: 15 mins**

Using delicate filo pastry makes these empanadas light and crispy on the outside, while the filling inside slowly melts into a scrumptious hot banana and chocolate mixture.

INGREDIENTS

about 8 sheets of filo pastry,
cut in half lengthways
melted butter or vegetable oil,
for brushing
2 ripe, sweet bananas
1–2 tsp sugar
juice of ½ lemon
175–200 g/6–7 oz plain chocolate,
broken into small pieces
icing sugar
and ground cinnamon, for dusting

NUTRITIONAL INFORMATION	
Calories 375	
Protein 5g	
Carbohydrate 57g	
Sugars 41g	
Fat 16g	
Saturates 8g	

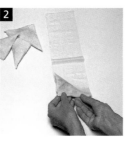

cook's tip

For a light and puffy effect, you could enclose the filling in sheets of ready-made puff pastry instead of filo, and bake in the same way.

1 Preheat the oven to 190°C/375°F/Gas Mark 5. Lay out a long rectangular sheet of filo on a clean work surface and brush with melted butter.

2 Peel and dice the bananas and place in a bowl. Add the sugar and lemon juice and stir well to blend, then stir in the chocolate. Place 2 teaspoons of the banana and chocolate mixture in one corner of the sheet of pastry, then fold over into a triangle shape to enclose the filling. Continue to fold in a triangular shape until the filo is wrapped around the filling. Dust the parcel with icing sugar and cinnamon and place on a large baking tray.

3 Repeat the process with the remaining sheets of filo and filling.

4 Bake in the preheated oven for 15 minutes, or until the pastries are golden. Remove from the oven, serve immediately and eat with care – the filling will be very hot.

sopaipillas

cook: 15 mins   **prep: 15 mins**   **serves 6**

These little, deep-fried puffs are popular sweet snacks in Mexico. You can serve them with honey, syrup, or simply sprinkled with a mixture of sugar and ground cinnamon.

NUTRITIONAL INFORMATION	
Calories	268
Protein	4g
Carbohydrate	50g
Sugars	21g
Fat	8g
Saturates	1g

INGREDIENTS

225 g/8 oz plain flour, plus extra for dusting

1 tbsp baking powder

pinch of salt

2 tbsp margarine, diced

175 ml/6 fl oz water

sunflower oil, for deep-frying

runny honey, to serve

cook's tip

Make sure that the oil heats up to its original temperature again after you have cooked one batch of sopaipillas, before adding the next.

1 Sift the flour, baking powder and salt into a bowl. Add the margarine and rub it in until the mixture resembles breadcrumbs. Gradually stir in the water and bring together to make a soft dough.

2 Turn out the dough on to a lightly floured work surface and knead gently until smooth. Roll out into a large, thin rectangle, then cut into 7.5-cm/3-inch squares.

3 Heat the oil in a large, deep frying pan to 180–190°C/350–375°F, or until a cube of bread browns in 30 seconds. Add the dough squares and cook in batches, until puffed up and golden, turning over to cook both sides. Remove the sopaipillas with a slotted spoon and drain well on kitchen paper.

4 Serve the sopaipillas warm, drizzled with a little honey.

tarte tatin

serves 8

prep: 15 mins, ⏲
plus 10 mins cooling

cook: 1 hr 5 mins ⏲

This upside-down apple tart has been a speciality of Sologne in the Loire valley for centuries, but was made famous by the Tatin sisters who ran a hotel-restaurant in Lamotte-Beuvron at the beginning of the twentieth century.

INGREDIENTS

225 g/8 oz shortcrust pastry, thawed if frozen

plain flour, for dusting

10 eating apples, such as Golden Delicious

4 tbsp lemon juice

115 g/4 oz unsalted butter, diced

115 g/4 oz caster sugar

½ tsp ground cinnamon

NUTRITIONAL INFORMATION	
Calories	348
Protein	2g
Carbohydrate	43g
Sugars	30g
Fat	20g
Saturates	11g

variation

If you can't find any Golden Delicious apples, Cox's apples will work just as well for this traditional French tart.

cook's tip

To achieve the best decorative effect when the tart is turned over, pack the halved apples in the tin with their cut sides facing up in Step 3.

1 Preheat the oven to 230°C/450°F/Gas Mark 8. Roll out the pastry on a lightly floured work surface into a 5-mm/¼-inch thick round, about 28 cm/11 inches in diameter. Transfer to a lightly floured baking tray and leave to chill in the refrigerator.

2 Peel, halve and core the apples, then brush with the lemon juice to prevent any discoloration. Heat the butter, sugar and cinnamon in a 25-cm/10-inch tarte tatin tin or heavy-based frying pan with a flameproof handle over a low heat, stirring occasionally, until the butter has melted and the sugar has dissolved. Cook for a further 6–8 minutes, or until the mixture is a light caramel colour. Remove from the heat.

3 Arrange the apples in the tin or frying pan, packing them in tightly. Return to the heat and cook for 25 minutes, or until the apples are tender and lightly coloured. Remove from the heat and leave to cool slightly.

4 Place the pastry over the apples, tucking in the edges. Prick the top and bake in the preheated oven for 30 minutes, or until golden. Leave to cool slightly, then run a knife around the edge of the tin to loosen the pastry. Invert on to a plate and serve warm.

teacup pudding

serves 4 **prep: 10 mins** ⏲ **cook: 3 hrs** ⏲

This is such an easy dessert to make, because all the ingredients, except the mixed spice, can be measured in the same cup. It tastes best served with a generous helping of warmed custard.

INGREDIENTS

butter, for greasing

1 cup self-raising flour

1 tsp mixed spice

1 cup soft brown sugar

1 cup shredded suet

1 cup currants

1 cup milk

custard, to serve

NUTRITIONAL INFORMATION

Calories	.....517 (per portion)
Protein	...............5g
Carbohydrate	.........72g
Sugars	..............46g
Fat	................25g
Saturates	.............14g

cook's tip

It doesn't matter whether you use a standard measuring cup (225 ml/8 fl oz) or an ordinary teacup to measure the ingredients, because the proportions remain the same.

1 Grease a 1-litre/1¾-pint pudding basin with butter. Sift the flour and mixed spice into a bowl and stir in the sugar, suet and currants, then add the milk and mix well. Spoon the mixture into the prepared basin.

2 Cut out a circle of greaseproof paper and a circle of foil 7.5 cm/3 inches larger than the rim of the basin. Place the paper circle on top of the foil circle, grease it, and pleat both circles across the centre. Place them over the basin, paper-side down, and tie around the rim with string.

3 Place the pudding basin on a trivet in a large saucepan and fill with boiling water to come halfway up the sides. Alternatively, place it in a steamer over a saucepan of boiling water. Steam for 3 hours, then carefully remove from the saucepan. Discard the covering, turn out on to a warmed serving dish and serve with custard.

creamed rice pudding

cook: 1 hr 5 mins   **prep: 5 mins**   **serves 4**

This rich, creamy rice dessert is a really comforting treat on cold winter days. You can serve it with a helping of canned or stewed fruit, or just enjoy it on its own.

NUTRITIONAL INFORMATION	
Calories	405
Protein	10g
Carbohydrate	73g
Sugars	42g
Fat	10g
Saturates	6g

INGREDIENTS

140 g/5 oz short-grain rice

1 litre/1¾ pints milk

115 g/4 oz sugar

1 tsp vanilla essence

TO DECORATE

ground cinnamon

cinnamon sticks

variation

For an orange flavour, omit the sugar and vanilla and stir 3 tablespoons of clear honey and the finely grated rind of 1 orange into the milk in Step 1.

1 Rinse the rice well under cold running water and drain. Pour the milk into a large, heavy-based saucepan, add the sugar and bring to the boil, stirring.

2 Add the rice, reduce the heat, cover and simmer gently, stirring occasionally, for 1 hour, or until the milk has been absorbed.

3 Stir in the vanilla essence. Transfer the rice to tall, heatproof glasses, sprinkle with a light dusting of ground cinnamon and serve immediately, decorated with cinnamon sticks.

bread & butter pudding

⏲ **cook: 50–60 mins**

🕐 **prep: 15 mins, plus 20–30 mins standing (optional)**

serves 6

NUTRITIONAL INFORMATION	
Calories	.427
Protein	.9g
Carbohydrate	.74g
Sugars	.63g
Fat	.13g
Saturates	.7g

variation

You can substitute sultanas for the raisins, and mixed spice for the ground cinnamon, if you prefer.

Everyone has their own favourite recipe for this traditional dish. This fruity version has added marmalade and grated apples to give the pudding a really rich and unique taste.

INGREDIENTS

5 tbsp butter, softened, plus extra for greasing

4–5 slices white or brown bread

4 tbsp chunky orange marmalade

grated rind of 1 lemon

85–125 g/3–4½ oz raisins

40 g/1½ oz chopped mixed peel

1 tsp ground cinnamon

1 Bramley apple, peeled, cored and roughly grated

85 g/3 oz light brown sugar

3 eggs

500 ml/18 fl oz milk

2 tbsp demerara sugar

cook's tip

This pudding can be left in the dish to cool completely before serving, if you wish – it tastes just as delicious served cold, with a helping of single cream.

1 Preheat the oven to 200°C/400°F/Gas Mark 6. Lightly grease an ovenproof dish with butter. Spread the slices of bread with butter, then spread the bread with marmalade.

2 Place a layer of bread in the base of the dish and sprinkle with the lemon rind, half the raisins, half the mixed peel, half the cinnamon, all of the apple and half the light brown sugar.

3 Add another layer of bread, cutting the slices so that they fit the dish.

4 Sprinkle over most of the remaining raisins and the remaining mixed peel, cinnamon and light brown sugar, sprinkling it evenly over the bread. Top with a final layer of bread, again cutting to fit the dish.

5 Lightly beat the eggs and milk together in a bowl, then sieve the mixture over the bread in the dish. If you have enough time to spare, leave the pudding to stand for 20–30 minutes.

6 Sprinkle the top of the pudding with demerara sugar and sprinkle over the remaining raisins. Cook in the preheated oven for 50–60 minutes, or until risen and golden. Serve.

autumn fruit bread pudding

serves 8 **prep: 10 mins,** ⏲ **plus 8 hrs chilling** **cook: 10 mins** ⏲

This is like a summer pudding, but it uses a selection of fruits, which are in season later in the year, such as apples, pears and blackberries, to make a succulent, sweet filling.

INGREDIENTS

900 g/2 lb mixed blackberries, chopped apples and chopped pears

150 g/5½ oz soft light brown sugar

1 tsp ground cinnamon

100 ml/3½ fl oz water

225 g/8 oz white bread, thinly sliced, crusts removed

NUTRITIONAL INFORMATION	
Calories	178
Protein	3g
Carbohydrate	42g
Sugars	31g
Fat	1g
Saturates	0.1g

variation

Try using thin slices of plain sponge cake instead of the bread. The sponge will turn an attractive pinkish colour from the fruit juices.

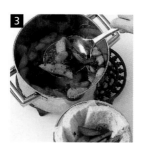

cook's tip

Stand the pudding on a plate when chilling in the refrigerator – this will catch any juices that run down the sides of the basin.

1 Place the prepared fruit in a large saucepan with the sugar, cinnamon and water. Bring to the boil, stirring, then reduce the heat and simmer for 5–10 minutes, or until the fruits soften but still hold their shape.

2 Meanwhile, line the base and sides of a 850-ml/1½-pint pudding basin with the bread slices, ensuring that there are no gaps between the pieces of bread.

3 Spoon the fruit into the centre of the bread-lined bowl and cover the fruit with the remaining bread.

4 Place a saucer on top of the bread to weigh it down. Leave the pudding to chill in the refrigerator for 8 hours, or overnight, then turn out on to a serving plate and serve immediately.

chocolate fondue

serves 4   **prep: 15 mins** ⏱   **cook: 5 mins** ⏱

This is a fun dessert to serve at the end of an informal meal. The fondue sauce can be prepared in advance, if you like, then warmed through and transferred into the fondue dish before serving.

INGREDIENTS

225 g/8 oz plain chocolate

200 ml/7 fl oz double cream

2 tbsp brandy

TO SERVE

selection of fresh fruit

white and pink marshmallows

sweet biscuits

NUTRITIONAL INFORMATION

Calories . . . . .536 (per portion)

Protein 4g

Carbohydrate 38g

Sugars 35g

Fat 40g

Saturates 25g

variation

Choose your favourite fruit to dip in the fondue. Kiwi fruit, banana chunks, apple pieces and strawberries go particularly well.

cook's tip

To prepare the fruit for dipping, cut larger fruit into bite-sized pieces. Fruit that discolours, such as bananas, apples and pears, should be dipped in a little lemon juice as soon as it is cut.

1 Break the chocolate into small pieces and place in a small saucepan with the cream. Heat the mixture gently, stirring constantly, until the chocolate has melted and blended with the cream.

2 Remove the saucepan from the heat and stir in the brandy.

3 Pour the mixture into a fondue pot or small flameproof dish and keep warm over a small burner.

4 Serve with a selection of fruit, marshmallows and biscuits for dipping. The fruit and marshmallows can be spiked on fondue forks, wooden skewers or ordinary forks for dipping into the chocolate fondue.

chocolate chip brownies

cook: 30–35 mins

prep: 25 mins, plus 30 mins cooling

makes 12

NUTRITIONAL INFORMATION

Calories	. . . .414 (per brownie)
Protein	. . . . .6g
Carbohydrate	. . . . .39g
Sugars	. . . . .24g
Fat	. . . . .27g
Saturates	. . . . .14g

variation

For extra flavour, stir in ½ teaspoon of vanilla essence when you add the nuts and white chocolate in Step 4.

Choose a good quality plain chocolate containing 70 per cent cocoa solids for these chocolate chip brownies. This will give them a rich flavour that is not overwhelmingly sweet.

INGREDIENTS

225 g/8 oz butter, softened, plus extra for greasing

150 g/5½ oz plain chocolate, broken into pieces

225 g/8 oz self-raising flour

125 g/4½ oz caster sugar

4 eggs, beaten

75 g/2¾ oz pistachio nuts, chopped

100 g/3½ oz white chocolate, roughly chopped

icing sugar, for dusting

cook's tip

Do not overcook the brownies – it won't be completely firm in the middle when it is removed from the oven, but it will set when it has cooled down.

1 Preheat the oven to 180°C/350°/Gas Mark 4. Grease a 23-cm/9-inch square baking tin and line with baking paper.

2 Place the chocolate and softened butter in a heatproof bowl set over a saucepan of simmering water. Stir until melted, then leave to cool slightly.

3 Sift the flour into a separate bowl and stir in the caster sugar.

4 Stir the beaten eggs into the chocolate mixture, then pour the mixture into the flour and sugar and beat well. Stir in the pistachio nuts and white chocolate, then pour the mixture into the tin, using a palette knife to spread it evenly.

5 Bake in the preheated oven for 30–35 minutes, or until firm to the touch around the edges. Leave to cool in the tin for 20 minutes. Turn out on to a wire rack. Dust the brownie with icing sugar and leave to cool completely. Cut into 12 pieces and serve.

rich chocolate loaf

serves 16

prep: 15 mins, ⟲
plus 1 hr chilling

cook: 5 mins ⟲

This rich chocolate surprise is incredibly easy to make. Its presentation as a simple, sliced loaf makes it an ideal idea for serving to casual guests as a teatime treat.

INGREDIENTS

75 g/2¾ oz almonds

150 g/5½ oz plain chocolate

6 tbsp unsalted butter

210 ml/7½ fl oz condensed milk

2 tsp ground cinnamon

75 g/2¾ oz amaretti biscuits, broken

50 g/1¾ oz no-soak dried apricots, roughly chopped

NUTRITIONAL INFORMATION	
Calories . . . . .189 (per slice)	
Protein 3g	
Carbohydrate 18g	
Sugars 18g	
Fat 12g	
Saturates 6g	

variation

Replace the amaretti biscuits with broken digestive biscuits and the apricots with the same amount of raisins, if you like.

cook's tip

Break the chocolate into small, manageable pieces before you heat it in Step 2. The smaller the pieces, the quicker it will melt.

1 Line a 675-g/1-lb 8 oz loaf tin with a sheet of foil. Roughly chop the almonds with a sharp knife and reserve until required.

2 Place the chocolate, butter, milk and cinnamon in a heavy-based saucepan. Place over a low heat, stirring constantly, for 3–4 minutes, or until the chocolate has melted.

3 Remove the saucepan from the heat and beat the chocolate mixture well. Stir in the almonds, biscuits and apricots with a wooden spoon, until well mixed.

4 Pour the mixture into the prepared tin and leave to chill in the refrigerator for 1 hour, or until set. Cut the loaf into slices to serve.

zabaglione

serves 6   **prep: 5 mins** 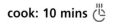   **cook: 10 mins**

This light and frothy, warm dessert which originates from Italy is a welcome treat at the end of a meal. You should serve zabaglione as soon as it is ready, to appreciate its full flavour.

INGREDIENTS

4 egg yolks

70 g/2½ oz caster sugar

125 ml/4 fl oz Marsala wine

amaretti biscuits, to serve

NUTRITIONAL INFORMATION	
Calories 110	
Protein 2g	
Carbohydrate 13g	
Sugars 13g	
Fat 4g	
Saturates 1g	

cook's tip

Decorate the zabaglione with a slit strawberry, placed on the rim of the glass, or serve with sponge fingers or crisp biscuits.

1 Half fill a saucepan with water and bring to the boil. Reduce the heat so that the water is barely simmering. Whisk the egg yolks and sugar with an electric whisk until pale and creamy.

2 Set the bowl over the saucepan of water. Do not let the base touch the surface of the water, or the egg yolks will scramble.

3 Gradually add the Marsala wine, whisking constantly with the electric whisk. Continue whisking until the mixture is thick and has increased in volume. Pour into heatproof glasses or bowls and serve immediately with amaretti biscuits.

flummery

⏲ **cook: 1 hr**　　　🕙 **prep: 10 mins, plus 2–3 hrs cooling/chilling**　　　**serves 4**

This charming, traditional English dessert looks pretty and tastes delicious. It would be a good choice as a cooling dish for a summer dinner party, and should be made well in advance.

NUTRITIONAL INFORMATION	
Calories	544
Protein	6g
Carbohydrate	45g
Sugars	20g
Fat	39g
Saturates	24g

INGREDIENTS

115 g/4 oz short-grain rice

300 ml/10 fl oz milk

300 ml/10 fl oz double cream, plus extra for decoration

55 g/2 oz caster sugar

1 tbsp grated lemon rind

1 tsp ground cinnamon, plus extra for dusting

cook's tip

If you have time, after rinsing the rice, soak it in cold water for 30 minutes, then drain. This helps the grains to absorb the liquid during cooking.

1 Rinse the rice well and place in the top of a double boiler with the milk, cream, sugar, lemon rind and ground cinnamon. Set over a saucepan of gently simmering water, cover and cook, stirring occasionally, for 55 minutes, or until most of the liquid has been absorbed and the rice is tender.

2 Remove the saucepan from the heat and transfer the rice mixture to individual dishes or cups. Leave to cool, then cover and chill in the refrigerator for 2–3 hours, or until set.

3 To serve, whip extra double cream, decorate each dish with a swirl and lightly dust with cinnamon.

syllabub

serves 6 **prep: 10 mins,** ⏲
plus chilling (optional) **cook: 0 mins** ⏲

Wine, brandy and cream make this old-fashioned dessert wonderfully self-indulgent – and it is guaranteed to make an impression if you serve it at a dinner party.

INGREDIENTS

175 ml/6 fl oz Madeira wine

2 tbsp brandy

grated rind of 1 lemon

125 ml/4 fl oz lemon juice

115 g/4 oz caster sugar

600 ml/1 pint double cream

10 amaretti biscuits or
ratafias, crumbled

ground cinnamon, for dusting

lemon slices, to decorate

NUTRITIONAL INFORMATION

Calories	635
Protein	. . . . .3g
Carbohydrate	. . . . .31g
Sugars	. . . . .31g
Fat	. . . . .52g
Saturates	. . . . .30g

cook's tip

Madeira is a fortified wine from the island of the same name. It may be dry, medium or sweet. Dessert Madeira is best for this recipe – use Bual or Malmsey.

1 Whisk the Madeira, brandy, lemon rind, lemon juice and sugar in a bowl until combined.

2 Add the cream to the bowl and continue whisking until the mixture is thick in consistency.

3 Divide the biscuits between 6 long-stemmed glasses or sundae dishes. Fill each glass or dish with the syllabub mixture and leave in the refrigerator to chill until ready to serve, if desired. Dust the surface of each dessert with cinnamon and decorate with lemon slices.

flambéed peaches

cook: 5 mins   **prep: 5 mins**   **serves 4**

This dessert is a fabulous end to a dinner party – especially if your guests are watching you cook. It makes a luxurious but, at the same time, refreshing final course.

NUTRITIONAL INFORMATION	
Calories	227
Protein	3g
Carbohydrate	26g
Sugars	26g
Fat	11g
Saturates	6g

INGREDIENTS

3 tbsp unsalted butter

3 tbsp muscovado sugar

4 tbsp orange juice

4 peaches, peeled, halved and stoned

2 tbsp almond liqueur or

peach brandy

4 tbsp toasted flaked almonds

cook's tip

Igniting the spirit will burn off the alcohol and mellow the flavour. However, if you are serving this dessert to children, you can omit the almond liqueur or brandy.

1 Heat the butter, muscovado sugar and orange juice in a large, heavy-based frying pan over a low heat, stirring constantly, until the butter has melted and the sugar has dissolved.

2 Add the peaches and cook for 1–2 minutes on each side, or until golden.

3 Add the almond liqueur and ignite with a match or taper. When the flames have died down, transfer to serving dishes, sprinkle with toasted flaked almonds and serve immediately.

sesame bites

serves 4   **prep: 15 mins** ⏱   **cook: 10–15 mins** ⏱

These delicious, Eastern-style deep-fried treats are crisp and nutty on the outside and melt-in-the-mouth on the inside. Serve them as a special mid-afternoon treat, or as party food.

INGREDIENTS

115 g/4 oz sugar

2 tbsp coconut milk

2 eggs, lightly beaten

2 tbsp coconut butter, melted

250 g/9 oz plain flour

4 tsp shredded coconut

¼ tsp baking powder

pinch of salt

4 tbsp sesame seeds

sunflower oil, for deep-frying

NUTRITIONAL INFORMATION	
Calories	.595
Protein	.11g
Carbohydrate	.80g
Sugars	.32g
Fat	.28g
Saturates	.12g

variation

If you have guests, arrange the bites on a serving plate and dust them with a little icing sugar to serve.

cook's tip

Make sure that you don't add too many of these sesame bites to the hot oil at once, as they will expand a little during cooking.

1 Combine the sugar, coconut milk, eggs and coconut butter in a bowl. Combine the flour, shredded coconut, baking powder and salt in a separate bowl, then stir the flour mixture into the egg mixture. Knead lightly until smooth.

2 Form the mixture into small balls with your hands, or with 2 teaspoons. Spread out the sesame seeds on a plate and roll the balls in them to coat.

3 Half-fill a wok or deep, heavy-based frying pan with oil and heat to 180–190°C/350–375°F, or until a cube of bread browns in 30 seconds. Add the sesame bites in batches, and deep-fry until golden brown. Remove with a slotted spoon and drain on kitchen paper. Serve warm.

fried bananas

serves 4   **prep: 10 mins** ⏲   **cook: 10 mins** ⏲

These wonderfully sticky battered bananas will bring out the child in every member of the family. You could serve them as a mid-afternoon treat or a late-night snack.

INGREDIENTS

115 g/4 oz plain flour	1 tbsp sesame seeds
½ tsp bicarbonate of soda	4 bananas
pinch of salt	groundnut or sunflower oil,
2 tbsp sugar	for deep-frying
1 egg	2 tbsp clear honey, to serve
6 tbsp water	

NUTRITIONAL INFORMATION	
Calories	.333
Protein	.6g
Carbohydrate	.62g
Sugars	.38g
Fat	.9g
Saturates	.1g

variation

You can use the same batter to coat slices of peeled and cored, fresh pineapple, and deep-fry them in the same way.

cook's tip

When deep-frying, never leave the frying pan unattended and always clean up any spills immediately. Leave the fried bananas to drain on kitchen paper to remove any excess oil before serving.

1 Sift the flour into a large bowl with the bicarbonate of soda and salt. Stir in the sugar, then whisk in the egg and enough of the water to make a smooth, thin batter. Whisk the sesame seeds into the batter.

2 Peel the bananas and halve them lengthways, then cut each one in half across the centre. Heat the oil in a wok or deep, heavy-based frying pan to 180–190°C/ 350–375°F, or until a cube of bread browns in 30 seconds.

3 Dip the banana quarters into the batter to coat, then deep-fry them in batches, until golden brown. Remove the fried bananas with a slotted spoon and drain on kitchen paper. Transfer to serving plates, drizzle with the honey and serve.

stuffed nectarines

🕒 cook: 40–45 mins   🕒 prep: 15 mins   serves 6

NUTRITIONAL INFORMATION

Calories	.260
Protein	.4g
Carbohydrate	.28g
Sugars	.27g
Fat	.10g
Saturates	.4g

variation

If you prefer, serve with ice cream instead of the whipped cream, and sprinkle the milk chocolate directly over the baked fruit and filling.

This delectable combination of juicy fruit, crunchy amaretti biscuits and continental chocolate is an irresistible summer treat, full of deliciously smooth, complementary flavours.

INGREDIENTS

85 g/3 oz plain continental chocolate, finely chopped

55 g/2 oz amaretti biscuits, crushed into crumbs

1 tsp finely grated lemon rind

white of 1 large egg

6 tbsp Amaretto

6 nectarines, halved and stoned

300 ml/10 fl oz white wine

TO DECORATE

whipped cream

55 g/2 oz milk chocolate, grated

cook's tip

Nectarines are an ideal fruit for stuffing and baking, because they have firm flesh, which holds its shape well during the cooking process.

1 Preheat the oven to 190°C/375°F/Gas Mark 5. Mix the plain chocolate, amaretti biscuit crumbs and lemon rind together in a bowl. Lightly beat the egg white in a clean bowl and add it to the mixture with half the Amaretto.

2 Slightly enlarge the nectarine cavities with a small, sharp knife. Add any removed nectarine flesh to the chocolate and crumb mixture and mix well.

3 Arrange the nectarine halves, cut-side up, in an ovenproof dish just large enough to hold them all in a single layer. Divide the chocolate and crumb mixture between them, piling it in the cavities. Mix the wine and remaining Amaretto and pour it into the dish around the nectarines.

4 Bake in the preheated oven for 40–45 minutes, or until the nectarines are tender. Transfer 2 nectarine halves to each individual serving plate and spoon over a little of the cooking juices. Serve immediately, decorated with a swirl of whipped cream and a generous sprinkling of grated milk chocolate.

rhubarb & apple crumble

serves 6   **prep: 15 mins**   **cook: 45 mins**

In this delicious, warming dessert, a mixture of rhubarb and apples is flavoured with orange rind, brown sugar and cinnamon and covered with a crunchy, hazelnut crumble topping.

INGREDIENTS

500 g/1 lb 2 oz rhubarb

500 g/1 lb 2 oz Bramley apples

grated rind and juice of 1 orange

½–1 tsp ground cinnamon

85 g/3 oz light soft brown sugar

CRUMBLE

225 g/8 oz plain flour

125 g/4½ oz butter or margarine

125 g/4½ oz light soft brown sugar

40–55 g/1½–2 oz toasted

chopped hazelnuts

2 tbsp demerara sugar (optional)

NUTRITIONAL INFORMATION

Calories	.516
Protein	.6g
Carbohydrate	.77g
Sugars	.45g
Fat	.22g
Saturates	.4g

variation

Any fruits can be topped with crumble. Other flavourings, such as 55 g/2 oz of chopped stem ginger, can be added to the fruit or to the crumb mixture.

cook's tip

This crumble can be served cold, if you prefer. Leave it in the dish to cool for 1–2 hours, then serve with a spoonful of whipped cream.

1 Preheat the oven to 200°C/400°F/Gas Mark 6. Cut the rhubarb into 2.5-cm/1-inch lengths and place in a large saucepan. Peel, core and slice the apples and add to the rhubarb with the grated orange rind and juice. Bring to the boil, then reduce the heat and simmer for 2–3 minutes, or until the fruit begins to soften.

2 Add the cinnamon and sugar to taste and transfer the mixture to an ovenproof dish. Make sure that the dish is no more than two-thirds full.

3 To make the crumble, sift the flour into a bowl. Add the butter and rub it in until the mixture resembles fine breadcrumbs.

Stir in the sugar, then the hazelnuts. Spoon the crumble mixture evenly over the fruit in the dish and smooth the top. Sprinkle with the demerara sugar, if liked.

4 Cook in the preheated oven for 30–40 minutes, or until the topping is golden brown, then serve.

warm fruit compote

serves 4   **prep: 10 mins** ⸦   **cook: 8–10 mins** ⸦

A bowl of warm summer fruits suffused with exotic spices releases a burst of flavours on to the palate. The velvety syrup is sure to make this fresh, sumptuous dish a firm favourite.

INGREDIENTS

4 plums, halved and stoned

225 g/8 oz raspberries

225 g/8 oz strawberries,
hulled and halved

2 tbsp muscovado sugar

2 tbsp dry white wine

2 star anise

4 cloves

1 cinnamon stick

NUTRITIONAL INFORMATION	
Calories 95	
Protein 2g	
Carbohydrate 21g	
Sugars 21g	
Fat 0g	
Saturates 0g	

1 Place all the ingredients in a large, heavy-based saucepan. Cook over a low heat, stirring occasionally, until the sugar has dissolved.

2 Cover tightly and simmer very gently for 5 minutes, or until the fruit is tender but still retains its shape. Do not let the mixture boil.

3 Remove and discard the star anise, cloves and cinnamon, and serve the compote warm.

cook's tip

These lightly cooked summer fruits will taste their best if you serve them with a helping of fresh single cream or plain vanilla ice cream.

clafoutis

cook: 45 mins

prep: 15 mins, plus 1 hr standing

serves 4

Although the many different recipes for this unusual, batter-based dessert may use a variety of fruits, cherries are the classic filling in Limousin in France, where the dish originated.

NUTRITIONAL INFORMATION	
Calories 297	
Protein 7g	
Carbohydrate 42g	
Sugars 31g	
Fat 11g	
Saturates 6g	

INGREDIENTS

450 g/1 lb sweet black cherries

2 tbsp cherry brandy

1 tbsp icing sugar, plus extra for dusting

butter, for greasing

BATTER

3 tbsp plain flour

3 tbsp sugar

175 ml/6 fl oz single cream

2 eggs, lightly beaten

grated rind of ½ lemon

¼ tsp vanilla essence

cook's tip

Traditionally, in Limousin, the cherries are not stoned before cooking, because the stones are thought to release extra flavour into the dessert.

1 Preheat the oven to 190°C/375°F/Gas Mark 5. Stone the cherries, then place in a bowl with the cherry brandy and icing sugar and mix together. Cover with clingfilm and leave to stand for 1 hour.

2 Meanwhile, grease a shallow, ovenproof dish with butter. To make the batter, sift the flour into a bowl and stir in the sugar. Gradually whisk in the single cream, beaten eggs, lemon rind and vanilla essence. Whisk constantly until the batter is completely smooth.

3 Spoon the cherries into the ovenproof dish and pour the batter over them to cover. Bake in the preheated oven for 45 minutes, or until golden and set. Lightly dust with extra icing sugar and serve warm, or leave to cool to room temperature before serving.

pancake pieces

cook: 10 mins   **prep: 15 mins**   **serves 4**

NUTRITIONAL INFORMATION	
Calories	306
Protein	. . . . .8g
Carbohydrate	. . . . .50g
Sugars	. . . . .26g
Fat	. . . . .10g
Saturates	. . . . .2g

variation

These pancake pieces are also delicious mixed with 400 g/14 oz of canned morello cherries in syrup, instead of the apricots.

This is a cheap and cheerful, easy-to-make dessert that is perfect for midweek family suppers, and surprisingly filling. Its casual presentation makes it a favourite with children.

INGREDIENTS

2 tbsp caster sugar

1 tsp ground cinnamon

125 g/4½ oz plain flour

pinch of salt

2 eggs, lightly beaten

125 ml/4 fl oz milk

400 g/14 oz canned apricot halves in syrup

sunflower oil, for brushing

cook's tip

Before you add the batter to the frying pan, make sure the oil is very hot. Tilt and roll the frying pan as you pour the batter in, to spread it over the base in a thin layer.

1 Place the sugar and cinnamon in a bowl, stir to mix and reserve. Sift the flour and salt into a separate bowl. Whisk the eggs and milk into the flour and continue whisking to make a smooth batter.

2 Drain the apricot halves, reserving the syrup, then whisk the syrup into the batter until combined. Roughly chop the apricots and reserve.

3 Heat a large crêpe pan or heavy-based frying pan and brush with oil. Pour in the batter and cook over a medium heat for 4–5 minutes, or until the underside is golden brown. Turn over with a fish slice or palette knife and cook the second side for 4 minutes, or until golden. Tear the pancake into bite-sized pieces with 2 spoons or forks.

4 Add the apricots to the pan and heat through briefly. Divide the pancake pieces and apricots between individual plates, sprinkle with the sugar and cinnamon mixture and serve immediately.

spiced steamed pudding

serves 6   **prep: 15 mins** ⏲   **cook: 1 hr 30 mins** ⏲

Steamed puddings are irresistible on a winter's day, but the texture of this pudding is so light it can be served throughout the year. It makes the ideal finale to a three course meal.

INGREDIENTS

125 g/4½ oz butter or margarine, plus extra for greasing

2 tbsp golden syrup, plus extra to serve

125 g/4½ oz caster sugar

2 eggs

175 g/6 oz self-raising flour

¾ tsp ground cinnamon

grated rind of 1 orange

1 tbsp orange juice

85 g/3 oz sultanas

40 g/1½ oz stem ginger, finely chopped

1 eating apple, peeled, cored and roughly grated

NUTRITIONAL INFORMATION

Calories 488

Protein 5g

Carbohydrate 78g

Sugars 56g

Fat 19g

Saturates 4g

variation

Substitute light brown sugar for the caster sugar or mixed spice for the cinnamon, if you prefer.

cook's tip

You can use an upturned saucer as a trivet when you steam the pudding in Step 5. Keep a kettle of boiling water handy for topping up the saucepan during cooking, otherwise it will boil dry.

1 Thoroughly grease a 850-ml/1½-pint pudding basin. Pour the golden syrup into the basin.

2 Beat the butter and sugar together until the mixture is light and fluffy and pale in colour, then beat in the eggs, one at a time, following each with a spoonful of the flour.

3 Sift in the remaining flour with the cinnamon and fold into the mixture with the orange rind and juice. Fold in the sultanas, then the ginger and apple.

4 Turn the mixture into the basin and smooth the top. Cover with a piece of pleated, greased baking paper, tucking the edges under the rim of the basin. Cover with a piece of pleated foil. Tie securely in place with string. Tie a piece of string over the top to make a handle.

5 Place the pudding basin on a trivet in a large saucepan half-filled with boiling water, cover and steam for 1½ hours, topping up with boiling water as necessary.

6 Remove the basin from the saucepan, remove the foil and baking paper and turn out on to a warmed serving plate. Serve immediately, in slices, with extra golden syrup.

blueberry compote

serves 6　　　**prep: 10 mins,** ↻ **plus 2–3 hrs chilling**　　　**cook: 5 mins** ↻

Serve this easy and attractive dish with whipped cream or ice cream and small, sweet, dessert biscuits. It is perfect for entertaining, as it has to be made in advance and chilled.

INGREDIENTS

675 g/1 lb 8 oz blueberries

280 g/10 oz caster sugar

1 tbsp water

2 tbsp gin

dessert biscuits, to serve

NUTRITIONAL INFORMATION

Calories 229

Protein 1g

Carbohydrate 57g

Sugars 57g

Fat 0g

Saturates 0g

1 Place the blueberries, sugar and water in a heavy-based saucepan over a low heat, shaking the saucepan occasionally, until the sugar has dissolved.

2 Remove the saucepan from the heat and gradually stir in the gin, then leave the mixture to cool completely.

3 Transfer the compote to dishes, cover and leave to chill in the refrigerator for 2–3 hours before serving with dessert biscuits.

variation

You can substitute fresh redcurrants for the blueberries and brandy for the gin, if you prefer.

apple fritters

cook: 4–6 mins

prep: 15 mins, plus 30 mins standing

serves 4

This is a very popular choice for family meals, as children and adults alike love the flavour and crispy texture of the apple rings – and you don't need a spoon or fork to eat them.

NUTRITIONAL INFORMATION	
Calories	437
Protein	7g
Carbohydrate	35g
Sugars	14g
Fat	31g
Saturates	18g

INGREDIENTS

115 g/4 oz plain flour

pinch of salt

2 egg yolks

1 egg white

1 tbsp sunflower oil

150 ml/5 fl oz milk

450 g/1 lb cooking apples

juice of 1 lemon

caster sugar, for sprinkling

115 g/4 oz unsalted butter

crème fraîche, to serve

cook's tip

Choose firm, tart apples for this dish, such as Bramleys or Granny Smith's. Once they are cut, they should be sprinkled with lemon juice immediately and cooked quickly to prevent any discoloration.

1 Sift the flour and salt into a mixing bowl. Make a well in the centre and add the egg yolks, egg white and oil. Gradually incorporate the flour into the liquid with a wooden spoon. Gradually beat in the milk and continue beating to make a smooth batter. Cover with clingfilm and leave to stand for 30 minutes.

2 Peel and core the apples, then cut them into rings about 5-mm/¼-inch thick. Spread them out on a plate and sprinkle with the lemon juice and caster sugar.

3 Melt the butter in a large, heavy-based frying pan over a medium heat. Dip the apple rings into the batter, one at a time, then drop them into the frying pan. Cook for 2–3 minutes on each side, or until golden. Transfer to a serving platter, sprinkle with more caster sugar and serve with crème fraîche.

caramelized oranges

serves 6

prep: 25 mins, ⟳
plus 1–2 hrs chilling

cook: 15–20 mins ⟳

These unusual, sugar-coated oranges look almost too pretty to eat – but make sure you do, because they taste wonderfully refreshing, with a real citrus tang.

INGREDIENTS

6 large oranges

5 tbsp water

100 g/3½ oz caster sugar

whipped cream, to serve

NUTRITIONAL INFORMATION

Calories	143
Protein	2g
Carbohydrate	35g
Sugars	35g
Fat	0g
Saturates	0g

cook's tip

For recipes using citrus peel, look for unwaxed specimens – that is, those that have not been treated with diphenyl to preserve their colour.

1 Carefully pare wide strips of rind from 2 of the oranges using a swivel-blade vegetable peeler. Cut the strips of rind into thin batons with a sharp knife and reserve a few for decoration. Peel all the oranges and remove traces of white pith. Cut the fruit horizontally into slices 1-cm/½-inch thick. Place in a serving bowl and tip in any spilt juice.

2 Before making the caramel, half-fill the sink with cold water. Place 3 tablespoons of water and all of the sugar in a heavy-based saucepan and bring to the boil, stirring constantly, until the sugar has dissolved. Boil, without stirring, until the syrup is a dark caramel colour. Remove the saucepan from the heat and carefully immerse the base in the cold water to prevent any further cooking.

3 Add the remaining 2 tablespoons of water to the saucepan with the orange rind and simmer over a low heat, stirring occasionally, for 8–10 minutes, or until the rind is almost translucent. Pour the mixture over the orange slices, turning them to coat.

Cool completely, then chill in the refrigerator for 1–2 hours. Serve with whipped cream, decorated with orange rind.

forest fruits granita

cook: 5 mins

**prep: 15 mins, plus
3–4 hrs cooling/freezing**

serves 4

*This is the perfect dessert for a hot summer's day. It's more
cooling and less calorie-packed than ice cream, but is packed
with a great combination of fruity flavours.*

NUTRITIONAL INFORMATION	
Calories 175	
Protein 2g	
Carbohydrate 44g	
Sugars 44g	
Fat 0g	
Saturates 0g	

INGREDIENTS

225 g/8 oz strawberries, hulled

175 g/6 oz raspberries

175 g/6 oz blackberries, plus extra
to decorate

1–2 tbsp lemon juice (optional)

140 g/5 oz caster sugar

150 ml/5 fl oz water

TO DECORATE

whipped cream

fresh mint sprigs

variation

For a really lazy granita,
replace the fruit purée with
1 litre/1¾ pints of fruit
juice, such as orange or
cranberry juice.

1 Place the strawberries,
raspberries and
blackberries in a blender or
food processor and process
to a purée. Push the purée
through a fine-meshed sieve
into a freezerproof container
to remove the seeds. Add
lemon juice to taste.

2 Place the caster sugar
and water in a small
saucepan over a low heat
and stir until the sugar has
dissolved. Pour the syrup over
the fruit purée and stir well to
combine. Leave to cool, stirring
occasionally, then cover and
place in the freezer for
2–3 hours, or until set.

3 Transfer the frozen
granita mixture into the
refrigerator 30 minutes before
serving. Spoon into tall glasses
or glass cups, and decorate
with whipped cream,
blackberries and fresh mint
sprigs. Serve.

saucy ice creams

⏱ cook: 5–10 mins

🕐 prep: 5–10 mins, plus 1 hr cooling/chilling

serves 6

NUTRITIONAL INFORMATION

Calories . . . . . . .52 / 369 / 103	
Protein . . . . .0 / 2 / 0g	
Carbohydrate . . . .11 / 29 / 10g	
Sugars . . . . .11 / 28 / 7g	
Fat . . . . .0 / 28 / 0g	
Saturates . . . . .0 / 17 / 0g	

variation

You can substitute other fruit such as pineapple rings or apricots for the apples, if you prefer.

Ice cream is a great freezer standby for dessert, but it can be a little dull and uninspiring. The best way to liven it up is to serve it with a selection of tasty, syrupy sauces.

INGREDIENTS

BERRY SAUCE

225 g/8 oz berries, such as blackberries

or raspberries

2 tbsp water

2–3 tbsp caster sugar

2 tbsp fruit liqueur, such as crème de cassis or crème de framboise

CHOCOLATE SAUCE

150 ml/5 fl oz double cream

55 g/2 oz unsalted butter

55 g/2 oz light muscovado sugar

175 g/6 oz plain chocolate, broken into pieces

2 tbsp rum (optional)

PORT SAUCE

350 ml/12 fl oz ruby port

2 tsp cornflour

cook's tip

All of the sauces taste spectacular served with plain vanilla ice cream, but ring the changes and try out lots of combinations to find out which sauce you prefer with your favourite flavoured ice cream.

1 To make the berry sauce, place all the ingredients in a saucepan over a low heat, stirring occasionally, until the sugar has dissolved and the fruit juices run. Purée with a hand-held blender or in a food processor, then push through a sieve into a bowl to remove the seeds. Add more sugar, if necessary. Serve warm or cold.

2 To make the chocolate sauce, pour the cream into the top of a double boiler and add the butter and sugar. Set over a saucepan of barely simmering water and stir until smooth. Remove from the heat, leave to cool slightly, then add the chocolate, stirring until melted. Stir in the rum (if using). Leave to cool to room temperature before serving.

3 To make the port sauce, place 50 ml/2 fl oz of the port in a bowl with the cornflour and stir to make a smooth paste. Pour the remainder of the port into a saucepan and bring to the boil. Stir in the cornflour paste and cook over a high heat, stirring, for 1 minute, or until thickened. Remove the sauce from the heat and leave to cool. Pour into a bowl, cover and chill in the refrigerator for 30 minutes before serving.

index

index